TO LASSO THE CLOUDS

MERCER UNIVERSITY PRESS

Endowed by

TOM WATSON BROWN
and
THE WATSON-BROWN FOUNDATION, INC.

TO LASSO THE CLOUDS
THE BEGINNING OF
AVIATION IN GEORGIA

DAN A. ALDRIDGE, JR.

MERCER UNIVERSITY PRESS · MACON, GEORGIA · 2016

MUP/ H916

© 2016 by Mercer University Press
Published by Mercer University Press
1501 Mercer University Drive
Macon, Georgia 31207
All rights reserved

9 8 7 6 5 4 3 2 1

Books published by Mercer University Press are printed on acid-free paper that meets
the requirements of the American National Standard for Information Sciences—
Permanence of Paper for Printed Library Materials.

ISBN   978-0-88146-574-7
Cataloging-in-Publication Data is available from the Library of Congress

To Judy

After these years of experience I look with amazement upon our audacity in attempting flights with a new and untried machine...

—Orville Wright

Contents

Image Credits

Teresa Laughlin Gensheimer: 1, 18

Glenn H. Curtiss Museum: 2, 3, 4

Buck Peacock Collection: 5

Hargrett Rare Book and Manuscript Library/University of Georgia Libraries (with permission of the Ben T. Epps family): 6, 7, 11, 12, 15, 19, 20, 21, 22, 26, 27, 28, 29, 30, 31, 32, 33, 34, 35, 36, 37, 38, 39, 40 (photograph by Robert Saye), 41 (photograph by Kenneth Kay), 42

Gary L. Doster Collection: 8, 10

Aviation Gazette (with permission of Ben T. Epps family): 9

Cradle of Aviation Museum: 13

Musée de l'Air et de l'Espace de Paris-Le Bourget: 14, 17

U.S.A. Studios: 16

Mary Jane Halyard: 23, 24, 25

Acknowledgments

The research for this project began in 2007 to compose a magazine article on the one hundredth anniversary of the first airplane flight in Georgia. But I soon began to have serious doubts that the first flight occurred in 1907 and further research was put on hold. It did not resume in earnest until 2009 when, in January of that year, I met Mary Jane Dulin Halyard of Orlando, Florida, Zumpt's grand-daughter. Mary Jane had a scrapbook with plane photographs on which Zumpt had typed narratives of what the photographs depicted. But she was not aware of Zumpt ever making a wood-framed, glass-covered collage of plane photographs.

That same month I made contact with Teresa Laughlin Gensheimer of Ohio, also one of Zumpt's granddaughters. Terri is the daughter of Mildred Ballenger Huff Laughlin, who was also liv-ing in Ohio and was ninety years old in January 2009. I asked Terri if she knew anything about Zumpt making a collage. She remembered her mother having a collage that fit the description of what I was looking for and thought it was possibly in a storage unit where a number of items were kept waiting to be cleaned out. Fortunately for the sake of history, she found the collage. It was in poor condition, with all the pictures and notes having fallen to the bottom of the frame, but the collage was retrieved and the notes and pictures preserved.

With this treasure trove of information it was clear this story merited much more than an article. The photographs and narratives I received from Mary Jane and Terri constitute a significant portion of this book, and I am indebted to them for sharing these items.

I am also indebted to the late Ben Epps, Jr., and the other children of Ben Sr., who preserved Ben Sr.'s scrapbook and the various papers and items of memorabilia that are now housed at the Hargrett Rare Book and Manuscript Library, University of Georgia

Libraries, in Athens, Georgia. The staff at the Hargrett Library was always friendly and professional every time I visited. They were most helpful in pulling materials from the Epps Papers collection and providing the majority of the images that appear in this book. The Hargrett Library was housed in the main library building at the University of Georgia when I began my research and is now in the new Russell Library Building, which is truly a world-class facility.

I also want to thank the staff in the main library at the University of Georgia, where the microfilm newspaper collection is located, for all the assistance I received from them.

During my research, I extensively relied on the collection in the Heritage Room of the Athens-Clarke County Library, in Athens. The staff there went out of their way to answer questions, show me how to use their equipment, and help locate items I needed.

A debt of gratitude is also owed to the staff of the Braselton Library, in Braselton, Georgia, my then hometown library, who helped locate books through the PINES System and arranged to have them shipped to Braselton from points all around the state of Georgia.

I was also assisted by the staff at the Jacksonville Public Library System, Jacksonville, Florida who searched their collection of the *Florida Times-Union* for Zumpt's obituary, which enabled me to locate his descendants.

Finally, I want to acknowledge the help I received from Pat Epps, Ben Sr.'s youngest son and an accomplished aviator himself. He gave me his time, furnished several pictures, and shared his family history. Pat is the image of his father.

TO LASSO THE CLOUDS

Ben Epps (left) and Zumpt Huff (right) with the Epps-Huff I Biplane on E. Washington Street, Athens, Georgia, May 13, 1909. Courtesy Teresa Laughlin Gensheimer.

Glenn H. Curtiss, "The Father of Naval Aviation" and "Founder of the American Aircraft Industry," Hammondsport, New York. Courtesy Glenn H. Curtiss Museum.

Members of the Aerial Experiment Association ("A.E.A.") in Hammondsport, New York: (left to right) Frederick "Casey" Baldwin, Chief Engineer; Army Lt. Thomas Selfridge, Secretary; Glenn Curtiss, Director of Experiments; Dr. Alexander Graham Bell, Chairman; and John A. D. McCurdy, Treasurer. Also in the picture is Augustus Post of the Aero Club of America (far right). Courtesy Glenn H. Curtiss Museum.

The A.E.A's "June Bug," flown by Glenn Curtis on its initial flight, July 4, 1908, becoming the first officially-recognized, pre-announced and publicly-observed flight in the U.S. Courtesy Glenn H. Curtiss Museum.

Bobby Walthour (left) with his pacer, Gussie Lawson (right). Courtesy Buck Peacock Collection.

Ben Epps with the Epps-Huff II Monoplane, June/July 1909, in front of Epps Garage at 120 E. Washington Street, Athens, Georgia. This is the "quintessential" photograph associated with the beginning of aviation in Georgia; however, this plane never flew. Courtesy Hargrett Rare Book and Manuscript Library/University of Georgia Libraries (with permission of Ben T. Epps family).

1907

Epps-Huff II Monoplane on Washington Street looking to the east. The multi-storied Southern Mutual Building is in the background (right). Courtesy Hargrett Rare Book and Manuscript Library/University of Georgia Libraries (with permission of Ben T. Epps family).

Epps-Huff II Monoplane on Washington Street looking to the east. The multi-storied Georgian Hotel is in the background (left). Courtesy Ernest Patrick Epps.

Epps-Huff III Monoplane in Lynwood Park, August 28, 1909, beginning its take-off run. Zumpt Huff watches (wearing black derby). Courtesy *Aviation Gazette* (with permission of Ben T. Epps family).

Epps-Huff III in Lynwood Park, August 28, 1909, proceeds with take-off. Courtesy Ernest Patrick Epps.

Epps-Huff III in Lynwood Park, August 28, 1909, after crashing into terrace. Courtesy Hargrett Rare Book and Manuscript Library/University of Georgia Libraries (with permission of Ben T. Epps family).

Zumpt Huff (center) in black derby hat inspects the damage to the Epps-Huff III after its crash in Lynwood Park, August 28, 1909. Courtesy Hargrett Rare Book and Manuscript Library/University of Georgia Libraries (with permission of Ben T. Epps family).

Walden III, piloted by Dr. Henry W. Walden. On December 9, 1909, after flying a distance of 30 feet, Walden was credited with flying the first monoplane in the U.S. Courtesy Cradle of Aviation Museum.

Blériot V: On April 5, 1907 Louis Blériot of France flew this plane a distance of 20 feet after a 305-foot run to become the first monoplane in the world to fly. Courtesy Musée de l'Air et de l'Espace de Paris-Le Bourget.

Blériot XI: Louis Blériot mailed this photograph to Ben Epps and Zumpt Huff in July 1909 shortly before he flew across the English Channel. Courtesy Hargrett Rare Book and Manuscript Library/University of Georgia Libraries (with permission of Ben T. Epps family).

Blériot XI: Louis Blériot flew this plane across the English Channel on July 25, 1909 to win £1,000 and making Blériot the first to fly across a large body of water. Courtesy U.S.A. Studios.

Louis Blériot (left) and Alessandro Anzani (far right) with the Blériot XI, July 1909.
Courtesy Musée de l'Air et de l'Espace de Paris-Le Bourget.

PLANE # 4-HERE BEN EPPS AGAIN REMODELED AIRPLANE # 3 , HE PLACED THE ENGINE AND THE PROPELLER IN FRONT.(IN 1909 GLENN CURTISS SUGGESTED HE PLACE THESE IN THE REAR, AS HE WAS DOING A PLANE was Building in New York. CURTISS HAD COME TO ATHENS TO CHECK ON BEN'S MOTORCYCLE AGENCY OF THE CURTISS MOTORCYCLE, THIS WAS THE ONLY HELP BEN RECEIVED FROM ANYONE CONNECTED WITH AVIATION THEN. IT Was AUGUST 31ST, WHEN HE MADE HIS FIRST FLIGHT, 1909.

THIS DIRT ROAD WAS ON THE EAST-
SIDE OF LYNNWOOD PARK, FROM THIS PARK BEN
MADE HIS FIRST FLIGHT AUGUST 31,1909. THE
GASOLINE ENGINE CAME OUT OF A MOTORCYCLE
BOBBY WALTHOUR, "THE WORLDS' CHAMPION BICYCLE
RIDERS OF THE WORLD, HAD BUILT IN FRANCE BY THE ANZANA MOTOR CO OF FRANCE
"BOBBY WALTHOUR "AT THE TIME WAS WORLDS CHAMPION BICYCLE RIDER" HAD THE MOTORCYCLE MADE FOR A PACE-MAKERHE SHIPPED IT HOME TO WALTHOUR & HOOD, BEN TRADED A TWO SEATED CADILLAC FOR THE MOTOR CYCLE FROM PALMER WALTHOUR, OF WALTHOUR & HOOD, ONE OF ITS FOUNDERS, AND A BROTHER OF BOBBY'S.

Epps-Huff V on Billups Street on the way to Lynnwood Park. Courtesy Teresa Laughlin Gensheimer.

Epps-Huff V in Lynwood Park. Courtesy Hargrett Rare Book and Manuscript Library/ University of Georgia Libraries (with permission of Ben T. Epps family).

Epps-Huff V after crashing in Lynwood Park. Courtesy Hargrett Rare Book and Manuscript Library/University of Georgia Libraries (with permission of Ben T. Epps family).

Epps-Huff VI in flight. Courtesy Hargrett Rare Book and Manuscript Library/University of Georgia Libraries (with permission of Ben T. Epps family).

Epps-Huff VI on unknown dirt road. Courtesy Hargrett Rare Book and Manuscript Library/University of Georgia Libraries (with permission of Ben T. Epps family).

James A. Huff family, taken on the day of Anabel Huff's funeral, 1902. Standing (left to right): Myrt, Zumpt. Seated (left to right): Floy, Nell, Kermit, J. A. Huff, Flossie. Courtesy Mary Jane Halyard.

1904 Cadillac on Ag Hill, Athens, Georgia, owned by Morton & Taylor Electrical. The first car driven by Ben Epps and Zumpt Huff. Seated in car: Everette P. Taylor (left) and Annie Griffeth (right). Courtesy Mary Jane Halyard.

Zumpt Alston Huff. Courtesy Mary Jane Halyard.

1912 Epps VIII Monoplane, first plane with ailerons. Courtesy Hargrett Rare Book and Manuscript Library/University of Georgia Libraries (with permission of Ben T. Epps family).

1914–1915 Epps IX Monoplane, with wing tip cut. Courtesy Hargrett Rare Book and Manuscript Library/University of Georgia Libraries (with permission of Ben T. Epps family).

1916 Epps X Biplane. Courtesy Hargrett Rare Book and Manuscript Library/University of Georgia Libraries (with permission of Ben T. Epps family).

Aeromarine, sea plane (the "flying boat") Springlake, New York. Courtesy Hargrett Rare
Book and Manuscript Library/University of Georgia Libraries (with permission of Ben T.
Epps family).

Monte Rolfe, 1919. Courtesy Hargrett Rare Book and Manuscript Library/University of Georgia Libraries (with permission of Ben T. Epps family).

Epps Air Field, June 1922 (left to right) Ben Epps, Grover Presnell, Doug Davis. Courtesy Hargrett Rare Book and Manuscript Library/University of Georgia Libraries (with permission of Ben T. Epps family).

Midget Car, the "Automobilette," built by Ben Epps in 1922. Courtesy Hargrett Rare Book and Manuscript Library/University of Georgia Libraries (with permission of Ben T. Epps family).

1924 Epps XI Light Monoplane, with 28 h.p. Lawrence engine (front view). Courtesy Hargrett Rare Book and Manuscript Library/University of Georgia Libraries (with permission of Ben T. Epps family).

1924 Epps XI Light Monoplane, sold July 1926, Syracuse, New York, (side view). Courtesy Hargrett Rare Book and Manuscript Library/University of Georgia Libraries (with permission of Ben T. Epps family).

1930

Ben Epps, Jr. (left), Ben Epps, Sr. (right), with Midget Car and Waco 9 (fall 1929). Courtesy Hargrett Rare Book and Manuscript Library/University of Georgia Libraries (with permission of Ben T. Epps family).

THE "FLYING EPPS FAMILY," OF ATHENS, GA. Left to right: Ben T. Epps, Sr.; Evelyn, 15; Ben Junior, 14; Mary Virginia, 11; James, 10; Charles, 5; George, 3; Mrs. Epps, and in front, little Douglas, 15 months old, named for Doug Davis, Atlanta pilot. Daddy Epps is Georgia's first pilot, having begun his flying in 1907, with a home-made plane. He now owns three airplanes, but his favorite is one he built entirely himself, with the exception of the Ford engine by which it is powered. Mr. Epps and Ben Junior do the piloting when the family goes for a sky-spin, but sister Evelyn is taking lessons from her brother and will soon be a ladybird.

The "Flying Epps Family" (left to right) Ben Epps, Sr., Douglas (in front of his father), Evelyn, Ben Jr., Virginia, Harry, Charles, George and Omie, with the 1930 Epps XII Light Biplane behind them. Courtesy Hargrett Rare Book and Manuscript Library/University of Georgia Libraries (with permission of Ben T. Epps family).

1930 **Epps XII Light Biplane, with Ford Model "A" engine, tested on June 13, 1930.** Courtesy Hargrett Rare Book and Manuscript Library/University of Georgia Libraries (with permission of Ben T. Epps family).

Epps Field, June 1931 (left to right) Harry Epps, Ben Jr., Ken Hamilton, John Burns, Ed Hamilton and Ben Sr. Courtesy Hargrett Rare Book and Manuscript Library/University of Georgia Libraries (with permission of Ben T. Epps family).

Doug Davis accepting the Unlimited Shell Speed Dash Trophy in Cleveland, Ohio, just hours before he died in the Cleveland National Air Races, September 3, 1934. Courtesy Hargrett Rare Book and Manuscript Library/University of Georgia Libraries (with permission of Ben T. Epps family).

March 3, 1935 crash behind residence on Lumpkin St., Athens, Georgia. Courtesy Hargrett Rare Book and Manuscript Library/University of Georgia Libraries (photograph by Robert Saye with permission of Ben T. Epps family).

October 16, 1937 crash at Epps Field. Courtesy Ernest Patrick Epps, (*Atlanta Georgian & News,* photograph by Kenneth Kay).

Benjamin Thomas Epps, Sr., 1931. Courtesy Hargrett Rare Book and Manuscript Library/ University of Georgia Libraries (with permission of Ben T. Epps family).

Prologue

A one-hundredth anniversary is cause for celebration. That's what took place on 20 October 2007 at the Georgia Center on the University of Georgia campus in Athens. The peak of leaf colors had passed a few weeks before, but there were enough reds and yellows clinging to branches as a reminder of the season. The football team had an open date that Saturday, but there was reason for the gathering crowd to be excited. In the still, crisp air, the sky glittered with stars. It was a perfect evening; not unusual for fall in this city.

The black-tie-optional crowd began arriving early for the one-hundred-dollar-a-plate dinner. The gala was a celebration of the one-hundredth anniversary of the first airplane to be built and flown in the state of Georgia. The featured item on the agenda was the presentation of the inaugural Ben T. Epps Aerospace Innovation awards, named in honor of the man who made that first flight and became Georgia's first aviator. Georgia's governor was slated to present the awards.[1]

Curiously, the host city's *Athens Magazine* celebrated the one-hundredth anniversary of Georgia's first flight a half year earlier during the winter to spring seasonal transition. Its March/April 2007 cover proclaimed, "100 years of Flight, Celebrating the Epps Legacy."[2]

Which of these celebrations was held in the actual season the first flight occurred? Did the first flight take place in early spring 1907, or did Ben Epps accomplish his historic feat in the fall of that year? Could it have taken place in one of the summer months so that both celebrations had the wrong season?

The state historical marker in front of the Athens-Clarke County-Ben Epps Airport terminal honors Ben Epps for being the first to fly in Georgia but doesn't provide the precise date of his flight.

The marker only notes, "Ben T. Epps designed, built and in 1907 flew the first airplane in the State of Georgia."[3] Similarly, the Georgia Aviation Hall of Fame in Warner Robbins, Georgia, where Ben Epps was one of the initial inductees in 1989, doesn't provide the precise date in his biographical information. Ben Epps's plaque states that he dropped out of Georgia Tech in 1906 and "[a] year later, he flew the first airplane in the State of Georgia."[4]

The precise date on which an event of this historical significance for the state occurred should be readily determinable. But for more than a century that has not been the case when it comes to pinpointing the date of the first airplane flight in Georgia.

In recent decades there have been numerous articles published about Ben Epps and the first flight. Yet not one of these articles provides the day, the month, or even the season in 1907 when this flight occurred. In November 2011, an article about the ceremonial placement of a bust of Ben Epps at Athens-Clarke County City Hall acknowledged, "The exact date and location [of the first flight] are unknown."[5] Perhaps just as curious, there are no articles that cite a primary source for the statement that the first flight took place in 1907.

During the one-hundredth anniversary year in 2007, one of the many articles commemorating this flight added, "Nobody knows exactly when it happened, *but we do know the year, 1907*" (emphasis added).[6] But how can we *know* if no primary source has ever been cited to establish that the first flight occurred in 1907?

During his lifetime, Ben Epps never gave a published interview, nor did he write or record in any other form his account of that first flight. However, after his death in 1937, three eyewitness accounts of that flight were published.

Hugh J. Rowe was the first to recount his memories of witnessing that flight in a recurring column he wrote for the *Athens Banner-Herald* called "Did It Ever Occur to 'U'." Rowe, born in Jackson County, Georgia, in 1869, was editor and proprietor of the

Athens Banner from 1897 to 1923, when the paper merged with the *Athens Herald* and he became editor of the *Athens Banner-Herald*. He continued as an editor in 1939 when he wrote his eyewitness account of Ben Epps's first flight.[7]

Shortly after Ben Epps's death, Rowe received suggestions from his readers that the airport in Athens be officially designated "Ben T. Epps Flying Field" to honor the late aviator. These suggestions prompted Rowe's 22 January 1939 column. He recalled, "Nearly a half century ago, the writer of this column was present [for Ben Epps's first flight]."[8] Rowe offered no more precise date. Obviously, his recollection was significantly off. A "half century ago" would have dated Ben Epps's first flight in 1889, fourteen years before Orville Wright took the world's first airplane flight.

Thomas W. Reed published the next eyewitness account ten years later in a column in the *Athens Banner-Herald*. Reed worked under Hugh Rowe as an editor for the *Athens Banner* from 1892 until November 1909, when he became registrar for the University of Georgia. Reed retired as registrar in 1945 and, in September 1947, began writing a column for the *Athens Banner-Herald* entitled "Echoes from Memoryland." His columns were reminiscences of people, places, and historic events in Athens.[9]

On 1 March 1949, Reed stated in his column that it was "about forty years ago" that he and Hugh Rowe, Reed's boss at the paper, were invited by Ben Epps to "witness the initial flight of his machine." Like Rowe, Reed did not provide the precise date of the flight, but his recollection would have placed the first flight "about" 1909.[10]

A third eyewitness account appeared in the *Atlanta Journal & Constitution* on 31 July 1966. Marion N. Todd of Winterville, Georgia, recalled that in 1905, when he was five years old, his father took him to visit Ben Epps's shop on East Washington Street in Athens where the plane was being built. Todd said it was "around

1908" when he saw Ben Epps's first flight, near Sandy Creek Bottoms in eastern Clarke County.[11]

None of these three eyewitness accounts gives the exact date of the first flight, nor do any of them state or suggest that it occurred in 1907. Neither Rowe nor Reed ventured to give a specific year, and Todd could only suggest that it was "around 1908." Americans remember the horrific terrorist attack on the United States that occurred on 9/11. Reminders of that day appear often in various media. But do *you* remember the year in which that happened? And just over a decade has passed since that attack. Keep in mind that Rowe, Reed, and Todd would have seen few, if any, reminders of the date of the first flight before their memories were put into print thirty to sixty years later.

Since mankind first saw a bird in flight, there have been dreams that one day flight would be possible for humans, too. Millenniums passed, and there were countless attempts before the world's first successful flight was made on 17 December 1903 at Kitty Hawk, North Carolina. It was one of the greatest achievements of the twentieth century. The year 1907 was only a handful of years removed from Orville Wright's achievement. For a teenager from Athens, Georgia, to duplicate the success of the Wright brothers only a few years later was a momentous event.

The 1903 Wright Flyer was a biplane, a fixed-wing aircraft with two main wings stacked one above the other. According to numerous articles, Ben Epps made his first flight in a monoplane—a fixed-wing aircraft with one main set of wing surfaces. A detail about Ben Epps's flight that has been overlooked in all the articles on this subject is that the *world's* first flight in a monoplane did not take place until 1907. A Frenchman, Louis Blériot, is credited with making the first flight in a monoplane, which successfully flew a short distance in April 1907.[12] If Ben Epps's flight took place in the early months of 1907, before Blériot's flight, then he could claim the title of first in the world to fly a monoplane. Even if Ben Epps's flight occurred in 1907 after

Blériot's flight, he still could claim the title of first to fly a monoplane in the United States. But no article has ever made this assertion.

There's no doubt that Ben Epps's flight drew a great deal of interest in Athens and across the state. Articles about his achievement attest to the fact that "a large group of citizens" witnessed his historic flight.[13] The *Atlanta Journal Magazine* recounted, "Most of Athens' sporting bloods and the idly curious were on hand...a crowd assembled."[14] With the allure of an historic event and a large crowd present, which included the proprietor and an editor of Athens's leading newspaper, how is it possible that no article on this event appears in any 1907 edition of the *Athens Banner*, or the state's largest circulated newspaper, the *Atlanta Constitution*, or any other newspaper in the state?

There is a simple answer to this question: the first flight did not take place in 1907. When the flight occurred early on a Saturday morning, the story was published the following Monday in the *Atlanta Constitution*. Reporters were present and documented the feat. It was such a big event that newspapers across the state ran the story. It was a source of tremendous pride for all Georgians—and at least one witness had a camera.

Shockingly, not one of the several published articles across the state announcing the first flight was ever cited or mentioned again. The story of the first flight in Georgia somehow became lost in newspaper archives and buried under the dust of aged recollections. The precise date of Ben Epps's first flight has not been reported in more than a hundred years. But even more egregious than this oversight is that not an ounce of credit has been given to the partner who worked side by side with Ben Epps in this quest. A century has passed since these two young men from Athens were last recognized as celebrities, being referred to as the "airship inventors"[15] and described by one newspaper as "a second pair of Wright brothers."[16]

For the first time since their successful flight, this book tells the complete story of the lives of these two pioneer aviators, the

5

formation of their partnership, their trials, tribulations, failures, and eventual success. Against all odds, they held tight to their dream and rode an unimaginable journey.

1

The Early Years

Benjamin Thomas Epps, Sr.

Benjamin Thomas Epps, Sr., was born on 20 February 1888 in Oconee County, Georgia, near McNutt's Creek, which separates Oconee and Clarke counties. He was the first of Thomas Jefferson Epps and Evelyn Langford Epps's ten children.[1] His parents were from the same area, which was the southwestern part of Clarke County at the time of their births; Oconee County was not created by the state legislature until 1875.[2]

Ben's parents married in Oconee County in October 1886. His father owned several large tracts of land in Oconee County, which he farmed, and operated a cotton gin and grist mill on McNutt's Creek.[3]

A second child, Ethyl Mae Epps, was born into the family in October 1889.[4] The family was still living in Oconee County the following year when Thomas Epps purchased fifty-six acres on the other side of McNutt's Creek in Clarke County.[5] Not long after this purchase, Thomas Epps moved his family across the creek, and they became residents of Clarke County.

One of Thomas Epps's first actions after moving into Clarke County was cosigning a petition to the Clarke County Ordinary Court (now known as the Probate Court) for the creation of a new militia district where his residence was located. A militia district, among other things, designates the boundaries of an election district in Georgia and is both named and numbered when created. As a result of this petition, on 1 February 1891, the Princeton District was created and designated as the 1467th Georgia Militia District.[6]

The purchase of the fifty-six acre tract in Clarke County was the first of several large tracts of land on the Clarke County side of McNutt's Creek that Thomas Epps would purchase during the ensuing years to expand his farm operation. He would become well known as one of Clarke County's leading farmers and was extensively involved in the affairs of the county.

In 1894, Ben turned six years old and was eligible to enroll in the Clarke County public school system. The only information available about Ben's early education is found in the biographical sketch authored by his oldest child and published in 1982 in the *Dictionary of Georgia Biography*. According to his daughter, Evelyn, Ben was educated in both the Clarke County public school system and the city of Athens public school system.[7] Ben's parents instilled in him the importance of an education, but the public education system available to him at that time left a lot to be desired.

The public school system in Georgia in the 1890s was still in its infancy. The state legislature first addressed the issue of a statewide, free, public education system in October 1870 by passing an act to establish a system of public instruction.[8] Under this act each county in the state constituted a school district that would oversee the education of its youth, who were to be educated in separate schools according to race. Each county was authorized to elect a school board that would have the authority to establish such schools as deemed proper, employ teachers, and furnish schoolhouses. The state funded this system through a number of revenue-generating mechanisms, including a poll tax, a special tax on shows and sale of liquors, gifts, and one-half of the net earnings of the state-owned Western & Atlantic Railroad. The funding mechanisms were estimated to generate an amount that could support a school system in every district in the state for at least three months per year.[9]

Three years after the enactment of the school law only thirty of Georgia's more than 130 counties had established a public school system.[10] Clarke County was one of the first counties to take advantage of the law, and on 7 January 1871, its residents elected their first school board.[11]

Despite a noble intent and no shortage of effort, the Clarke County Board of Education struggled from the start in its efforts to build an educational system of which its residents could be proud. The education funds that Clarke County received from the state were woefully inadequate, averaging about one dollar per pupil. Teachers found it difficult to live off what they were being paid and often had to endure significant delays before receiving their payment. As a result, the school board had difficulty attracting competent, qualified teachers.

There were also no funds available to construct or buy school-houses, so privately owned facilities had to be found in each of the militia districts in Clarke County that could be used. These were generally one-room structures, staffed by a single teacher, and most were inadequate at providing a suitable learning environment. The lack of funding also meant that the schools could only remain open on a free basis for three months. After that, the school either closed for the year or remained open only for the students who could afford to pay tuition.

Enrollment in the public school system was voluntary. That fact, coupled with the widespread negative feelings toward the system, meant a low attendance. Rarely did more than 50 percent of school-age children enroll, and the percentage that actually attended was even lower.[12]

The system was the subject of harsh criticism from county residents. Its shortcomings prompted grand juries, which investigated the affairs of the county, to "heartily condemn" the public school system.[13]

The residents of the city of Athens had similar negative feelings about the county public school system. City residents responded by voting, in November 1885, to establish the Athens Public School System, separate and apart from the county system.[14] The Athens

Board of Education began its first school year in September 1886,[15] offering the youth of the city a longer yearly school term than the county and a graded system that included high school grades.[16]

In 1894, Ben was of age to attend first grade. By this time the city school system had expanded to six schoolhouses: four for white students and two for black students. The white schools offering a first grade were Meigs Street, Oconee Street, and Baxter Street.[17] Ben's family was still living in the county on Epps Bridge Road. Although Clarke County residents could attend a school in the city's system, the nearest city school to Ben's house would have been almost four miles away. It would have been a long walk or wagon ride for Ben to attend the closest city school. Ben also had a younger sister and brother, with a third sibling on the way by that time, all vying for their parents's time and attention. Although there is no source for the specific school where Ben began his formal education, it was likely the county school most convenient to his home.[18]

By 1894 the school term in the county school system had been increased from three to five months. In the year Ben started school, Clarke County still had not constructed a schoolhouse and did not own any buildings. The branches of study offered were reading, writing, arithmetic, spelling, English grammar, geography, and history.[19]

At the April term in 1896, the grand jury recommended for the first time that funds be appropriated from the general expense account of the county and given to the board of education for the building of schoolhouses.[20] By November 1896, the board of education held the deeds to four schoolhouses, one of which was the Princeton schoolhouse in the Princeton Militia District, where Ben's family resided.[21] There is no indication that Ben ever attended this school and there may have been another county school closer to his residence.

With the approach of a new century, Ben was ready to start high school. The county school system still did not offer high school grades and only operated on a five-month school term. By contrast, the city school system operated a nine-month school term and offered high school grade levels. High school grades were taught to white students at the Washington Street School, which was an attractive two-story, brick building. The girls occupied the lower floor and the boys the upper floor. The building was constructed on the block in downtown Athens now bounded by Washington Street, College Avenue, Hancock Avenue, and Jackson Street.[22] Washington Street School was the largest school in the city system and the only school for white students that offered seventh, eighth, and ninth grades.[23]

Ben was of age to attend seventh grade in fall 1900. Based on the biography written by his daughter that states Ben received part of his education in the city of Athens school system, it's likely he transferred into the city school system when he started seventh grade.

A decade after it was created, the Athens school system was praised as one of the best in the state.[24] But despite glowing performance accolades, attendance in the city schools was only slightly better than in the county schools; attendance remained voluntary. In the year that Ben was in seventh grade, only 62 percent of the white school-age population attended.[25]

When the doors to Washington Street School opened in September 1902, it marked the beginning of Ben's ninth grade year and his final year in the city school system.[26] That fall there were twenty-four students on the ninth grade roll at Washington Street School. Graduation exercises for this high school class were held on 27 May 1903 in the opera house, located across the street from the school, and eighteen graduates listened to a brief address and then received their diplomas. The *Athens Banner* described the ceremony and named each graduate, but Ben's name was not listed as one of these eighteen.[27] Ben either graduated before May 1902, did not receive a diploma, or his name was inadvertently omitted from this article.

Although few specifics are known about Ben's elementary and secondary school education, his post-secondary education is documented. In fall 1903, Ben was attending college in Atlanta. At fifteen years of age, which was not an unusually young age to attend college at the time, he was enrolled at the Georgia School of Technology, more popularly known as Georgia Tech.[28] From the outset, Ben was concerned about the amount of money his parents were spending to send him to Georgia Tech; money that he well knew they needed to feed and clothe his now six brothers and sisters back home.

Ben's board was fifteen dollars a month, due on the first of each month, and he wrote to his parents asking them to send his board money for November 1903. When he did not receive a response, he wrote them again on 6 November to remind them to send the board money right away, so he could avoid "a lot of trouble." His letter also noted that the weather was turning cold. He'd found a wool sweater for $1.00 that he wanted to buy, and he needed to get his teeth fixed "as they are getting bad," but then he added, "I hate to ask you for money."[29]

Ben was back at Georgia Tech in fall 1904, a little homesick, exchanging letters with his parents. The subject in a December 1904 letter to his parents was not another reminder to send his board money, but rather about his concern as to whether he should remain at Georgia Tech. He was not doing as well in his coursework as he had hoped and "did not want to continue to use [his parents's] money when it could be put to a better advantage." Exams were about to begin, and after finishing his last exam, Ben planned to return home on Friday, 23 December, on the 8:00 P.M. train from Atlanta to Athens. Over the Christmas holidays he wanted to discuss with his parents whether he should drop out of school. He closed this letter stating, "Please write more often. Your son, B. T. Epps."[30]

The decision that Ben would not return to school at Georgia Tech in January was apparently made quickly. Not one to remain idle, and aided by his father's contacts with many local businessmen, Ben found a job in Athens and reported to work the first week in January 1905. He was sixteen years old, with a birthday coming up in February.

The first day on his new job, Ben met another teenager, a coworker, with the most unusual first name he'd ever run across: Zumpt Huff.

Zumpt Alston Huff

Zumpt Alston Huff was born in the Mason Mill and Bluestone Creek area of Madison County, Georgia, on 27 September 1889. He was the eldest of six children born to James Albert Huff and Annabel Wilbanks Huff. It was Zumpt's mother who came up with his forename, telling him she found the name in the Bible. But neither Zumpt nor anyone he asked was ever able to find a "Zumpt" in the Bible.[31]

Both of Zumpt's parents were born in the Millstone Creek area of Oglethorpe County, Georgia, and both were fourth-generation descendants of families who had settled in Oglethorpe County by 1800, making their families some of the earliest settlers in the county. According to family history, the Huffs came to Georgia from Virginia after the American Revolution, settling first in Wilkes County and later in Oglethorpe County. Zumpt's father was the seventh of eight children. He was four years old when his father, Zumpt's grandfather, John Peter Huff, was killed. John Peter Huff died at Cold Harbor, Virginia, on 27 June 1862, while serving as a private in the 38th Regiment, Georgia Volunteer Infantry, in the Civil War.[32]

Zumpt's maternal grandfather, William Harrison Wilbanks, was also a Confederate veteran. He served three years with Walker's Precinct, Company D, 41st Tennessee Regiment, before being captured by Union soldiers while on leave to visit a sick family member in Lincoln County, Tennessee, in December 1864. He was held prisoner in Nashville until the end of the war.[33]

It was in Madison County, Georgia, that Zumpt's parents met and later married on 14 October 1888.[34] Annabel was a schoolteacher in Madison County's public school system, teaching in a one-room schoolhouse. The Madison County school system at that time was experiencing the same growth struggles and lack of funding that Clarke County's rural school system was undergoing. As a young man, Zumpt's father farmed, but he later learned the art of photography, and by the time of his marriage to Annabel, he made his living with a camera taking portrait photographs.[35]

James Huff's photography business required him to do a great deal of traveling. Over the years after Zumpt's birth, the family moved from Madison County to Stephens County, Franklin County, Clarke County, and Oglethorpe County, Georgia. They also lived for brief periods in Fort Hill, Clemson, and Honea Path, South Carolina. Zumpt would have been of age to attend first grade in 1895. At that time the family was living in Toccoa, Stephens County, Georgia. With his family moving as often as it did, there would not have been any one school in which Zumpt could have received his elementary education. It is likely that Zumpt received most, if not all, of his education at home from his mother, a former teacher.

At the time of the 1900 United States Census, Zumpt was ten years old and living with his father, mother, and four sisters in Carnesville, Franklin County, Georgia. The family rented a house across the street from the Carnesville Methodist Church. According to census records for that year, Zumpt was able to read and write; however, he had not attended a school that year. His sister, Myrtle, who was eight years old and the oldest of his sisters, was able to read and write and attended school for five months in 1900 in the Franklin County school system. Despite being only ten years old, Zumpt worked full time. His occupation on the census records lists him as a "farm laborer" and shows that there were only two months that year when he was not working.[36]

At the turn of the century there was no city school system in Franklin County, only the county school system. As was the case with the Clarke County school system, Franklin County did not offer high school grades. As a result, attending high school was not an option available to Zumpt. There is no evidence that he was ever enrolled in a school system after his tenth birthday.

In 1901, Annabel gave birth to Zumpt's only brother, Kermit Theodore Huff. Some nine months later, after a brief illness, Annabel died on 30 May 1902, at the age of thirty-three. According to family history she suffered from an intestinal disorder.[37]

Annabel was buried in the cemetery behind Carnesville Methodist Church. On the day of her funeral, Zumpt's father decided to capture the moment on film. He had all the children pose with him for a family portrait. The photograph shows Zumpt as a handsome young boy, with thick, jet-black hair, standing behind his seated father. Every face in the photograph reflects the loss of Annabel (Image Number 23).

Left with six children, ages nine months to eleven years, James Huff was not able to continue his photography business and raise his children at the same time. He split the children up and sent them to live with various relatives until he was in a better position to care for them.

On 1 July 1903, James Huff remarried, exchanging vows with Annabel's younger sister, Alice Salinda Wilbanks, in Franklin County. After his remarriage, James brought all of his children back to live with him and his new wife. A year later, James and Alice had their only child together, Gaylor Jane Huff, born on 15 August 1904. It was around this time that James Huff decided to move the family to Athens. They rented a house on Baxter Street, just up the hill from the intersection with Lumpkin Street.[38]

Athens had a significantly larger population than Carnesville. According to a census taken in 1904, the city of Athens had just over 13,100 residents.[39] The Athens market offered greater potential for portrait photography and was a market that James Huff had not previously tapped. While he promoted his photography business in Athens, he also began to develop a new business interest.

Within a year or two of moving to Athens, James Huff began manufacturing and selling a tonic he called "Huff's Balm of Gilead." He registered his tonic with the U.S. Food and Drug Administration on 30 June 1906. He also received a permit from the Ordinary Court of Clarke County on 5 October 1907, allowing him to make and sell his tonic. He advertised his "Balm of Gilead" tonic in local newspapers as "a wonderful blood purifier and health restorer, a cure for *all* diseases."[40] The *Athens City Directory*, 1909, lists James Huff's occupation as "medicine vendor."[41]

After moving from a rural farming community to the city, Zumpt no longer worked as a farm laborer. He was in search of a new job. Athens was a growing city with an impressive mix of commercial enterprises. It was one of the largest cotton markets in the state, averaging 80,000 bales a season, and was recognized as having an enormous wholesale trade, especially in groceries, dry goods, and hardware. There were four railroads that entered Athens, and the city had one of the most complete and up-to-date electric street railway systems in the United States. It was said that there was no city in the state making as rapid strides in a business and industrial way as Athens. Jobs were plentiful for young men starting careers.[42]

Before the end of 1904, Zumpt, who was then fifteen years old, became employed by Morton & Taylor Electrical Contractors. Morton & Taylor Electrical was a brand new company, which formally announced its opening on 11 January 1905. The business was located at 7 College Avenue in the Commercial Hotel building in downtown Athens. It was owned and operated by Joseph Morton and Everett P. Taylor.[43]

The company did all kinds of electrical contracting work, sold electric, gas, and combination fixtures, arc lamps, incandescent lamps, electric motors and generators, dynamos, and, during the Christmas season, sold electric lights for Christmas trees. They also repaired electric motors and generators. The company advertised that no contract was too large or too small for them to handle.[44] Before the end of 1905, Morton & Taylor Electrical was also advertising as an agent for Rambler, Yale, and Cadillac automobiles.[45]

During the first week in January 1905, sixteen-year-old Ben Epps walked through the door of Morton & Taylor Electrical and introduced himself to Zumpt Huff as the company's newest employee.

2

Birth of a Partnership

The natural talent that Ben and Zumpt possessed when it came to
working with their hands on all things electrical and mechanical
developed and flourished at Morton & Taylor Electrical. It was a
talent that both possessed in abundance and displayed in their
vocations for the rest of their lives. They were particularly fascinated
by automobiles, which were just beginning to appear on the streets of
Athens.

Ben and Zumpt experienced first-hand the introduction of the
automobile to the citizens of Athens. Since Morton & Taylor
Electrical served as an agent for automobiles, the company provided
them with the opportunity to drive what was purported to be the
fourth automobile in Athens. The car was a 1904 Cadillac, two-
seater, owned by their employer. The engine was a single cylinder,
chain drive, with a top speed of thirty miles per hour. It sold for $950.
Zumpt kept a photograph of this car with Everett P. Taylor and
Annie Griffeth seated in it on Ag Hill, at the corner of Lumpkin and
Cedar streets (across Lumpkin Street from present-day Oglethorpe
House, Image Number 24). Although Annie Griffeth was with
Everett Taylor on that occasion, fewer than seven years later he would
marry Zumpt's oldest sister, Myrtle.[1]

It's not known how long Ben and Zumpt worked at Morton &
Taylor Electrical, or exactly what became of this company. The
company advertised heavily in the newspaper in 1905 and for the first
eight months of 1906, but no advertisements ran after 30 August
1906.[2] At some point between September 1906 and January 1908,
Morton & Taylor Electrical ceased operations. Joseph Morton

married in Toccoa, Georgia, on 29 January 1908 and stayed in Toccoa to live.[3] Everett Taylor remained in Athens and on 2 June 1908 began advertising his new business, "E. P. Taylor, Everything Electrical," located at 198 College Avenue.[4] Taylor Electric Company remained in operation for many years thereafter. Ben and Zumpt may have worked for this new company after Morton & Taylor Electrical ceased operating, but if they did, it was only for a few months.

After leaving Morton & Taylor Electrical, Zumpt's next documented employment was with the Crystal Theatre. He was working as an assistant projector operator with this motion picture theater, which was located at 187 North Lumpkin Street, at least by the end of 1908.[5] According to Ben's biography, he started his own business in 1907, an electrical contracting service and garage, at 120 East Washington Street.[6] However, this date is not correct. Ben did not have a business at 120 East Washington Street in 1907 or for at least the first eleven months of 1908.

W. H. Bishop Motor Cars and Supplies was the business operating at 120 East Washington Street in 1908.[7] As late as 15 November 1908, the *Athens Banner* ran an advertisement for the manager of W. H. Bishop, who was selling two Winchester shotguns at his employer's business at this same address.[8] But by 1909, Bishop Motor Cars was advertising in the *Athens Banner* at its new location on Clayton Street[9], which was also listed in the *Athens City Directory*, 1909.[10]

After Bishop Motor Cars vacated the premises at 120 East Washington Street near the end of 1908, Ben moved in. He hung a shingle above the door advertising "B. T. Epps Electric Contractor." Another signboard cantilevered from the brick façade of the building promoting Ben's "Garage."

Ben offered a variety of services from this location. The *Athens City Directory*, 1909, listed his business under the following categories: Automobiles & Supplies, Automobile Repairing, Electrical Dealers & Contractors, Garages—Auto, and Locksmith. The primary service listing for the business in the list of "Athens Businesses" was Electrical Dealers & Contractors. Ben's occupation under the "Individuals" listed in Athens was "electrical contractor, locksmith."[11]

Ben was twenty years old by December 1908, when he opened his business on East Washington Street. He was living with his parents and eight brothers and sisters inside the city limit of Athens. In the early 1900s, Thomas Epps expanded his farming operations in Clarke County by purchasing over 350 acres on the Middle Oconee River. He built a mill and country store on the property that fronted on Epps Bridge Road.[12] In addition, he bought a lot at 1020 West Hancock Avenue where he built a house. Shortly thereafter, in November 1906, he bought the one-acre lot that was directly behind this property. This lot was located on the southwest corner of Meigs and Franklin streets. Thomas Epps did not become a resident of Athens before the deadline for registering to vote in the fall 1906 city elections, but he and his family became residents of the city of Athens not long thereafter.[13]

At the time Ben opened his business on East Washington Street, too, was living with his family: his father, stepmother, four sisters, a brother, and his five-year-old half-sister. The Huffs were still renting the house at 280 Baxter Street.[14]

Ben's move into the building at 120 East Washington Street marked the beginning of the Epps-Huff partnership. By this time Ben and Zumpt's natural talent for working with their hands on all types of mechanical devices was evident. They also shared a fascination and passion for bicycles, motorcycles, and automobiles. Bicycles became a national craze in the 1890s, and a few years into the twentieth century, motorcycles and automobiles began to appear in Northeast Georgia.

Ben's career path in particular was remarkably similar to that of the Wright brothers in Dayton, Ohio. The Wrights enhanced their mechanical skills in businesses that involved motors, machinery, and the sale and repair of bicycles. Their work with bicycles was especially influential in their pursuit to balance and control an unstable flying machine.[15]

Ben and Zumpt's interest in different modes of transportation was a natural lead-in to travel by means of a flying machine, and the Wright brothers were their inspiration for a dream that would permanently bond them to Georgia's pioneer aviation history. If the Wright brothers could build a heavier-than-air machine that was capable of sustained, controlled flight, then surely they, possessed with the exuberance of youth, could do the same. They would build an airplane that would allow them to join the red-tailed hawks that circled effortlessly among the clouds in the Northeast Georgia sky.

Ben and Zumpt began work on their dream at the end of 1908.[16] They started without any formal education or training in aeronautics, but they possessed a zeal that was fueled by pictures, mechanical drawings, and published articles detailing the Wright brothers' progress and technical advances in how they were able to make their machine fly. This information was available in trade magazines such as *Popular Mechanics* and *Science*.[17] Ben had subscriptions to some of these periodicals and liked to read all of the technical information he could find.[18]

The first plane constructed by the Epps-Huff partnership was designed after the 1903 Wright Flyer. Like the Wright Flyer, it was a biplane, a fixed-wing aircraft with two superimposed wings; one wing above and parallel to the other. It was constructed of wood, wires, and fabric. Inter-plane struts that divided the wings into bays connected the upper and lower wings, or "planes," which were braced by diagonal wires. The wires that ran outward from the upper to the lower plane acted to resist the distortion on the bay from gravity. These wires were called landing wires. The wires that ran from the lower "plane" outward to the upper "plane" acted to resist distortion under the aerodynamic lifting force and were referred to as lifting wires. The resulting combination of struts and wires made the structure quite rigid.

An elevator was positioned in front of the biplane's body. It was a two-plane, rectangular-shaped structure that could be tilted up or down. Extending from the rear of the biplane was a flat, single-plane rudder that could be maneuvered from side to side.

In order to control the flight of their biplane, Ben and Zumpt had to manage the three axes that the Wright brothers successfully managed with their 1903 Wright Flyer: pitch, yaw, and roll. Pitch is the motion of the nose and tail of the aircraft up and down, which is controlled by the elevator. Yaw is the side-to-side directional changes of the nose of the aircraft, which is controlled by the rudder. Roll is the motion of the wing tips up and down. Like the Wright Flyer, Ben and Zumpt's biplane used wing warping to control the roll. This technique, which was patented by the Wright brothers, used a system of pulleys and cables to twist the trailing edges of the wings, up and down in opposite directions, allowing the pilot to maintain lateral control of the aircraft.

Ben and Zumpt spent the winter months of 1909 in the East Washington Street garage assembling their biplane. They worked nights and on weekends after Ben finished his work at the garage and Zumpt got off from his work around the corner at the Crystal Theatre. They built the wooden frame and wings then strung wire cable to hold it all together. The two wings, the elevator, and the rudder were covered in fabric that was stitched together on Ben's mother's sewing machine at home.[19]

On 13 May 1909, their biplane, which for purposes of reference is designated as the Epps-Huff I, was ready to make its public debut. Ben and Zumpt carried their prized biplane out to the clay street in front of the garage and placed it on wooden crates to be photographed. The wheel undercarriage was not yet attached, nor had the engine or propeller been installed at the time of this photograph. Both Ben and Zumpt posed for the camera in front of their biplane.

Ben, dressed in dark wool pants held up by suspenders, with the sleeves of his white cotton shirt rolled up, was wearing a wool news-boy cap. Zumpt stood to the left of Ben, dressed in a mid-thigh, black wool coat and was wearing a black felt derby hat pushed back on his head (Image Number 1). They were joined on the street by a reporter for the *Athens Banner*, who did not appear in the photograph but was asking questions and taking notes.

If the citizens of Athens were not yet aware of the new partnership that Ben and Zumpt had formed to build the first airplane in Georgia, they were informed the following day when the paper proclaimed, "Two Athens Boys Building Airship."

> Two Athens boys, Messrs. Zump [*sic*] Huff and Ben Epps, are now engaged in the work of building an airship. They took the ship out on Washington street yesterday afternoon and had it photographed....
>
> The two young men, who have considerable mechanical talent, are confident that they will be able to complete a ship that will fly through the air. They will have it ready for its trial trip within the next few weeks.
>
> The progress of their work will be followed with interest, as this is the first attempt to build an airship in Georgia.[20]

Like the 1903 Wright Flyer, the Epps-Huff I was a pusher-type design in which the propeller faced aft (rearward) and acted to push the plane forward. The propeller was to be installed behind the two fixed-wings. Ben and Zumpt used the pusher-type design for their biplane based on a suggestion that Ben received from Glenn H. Curtiss, a well-known pioneer aviator from New York.

When Ben established his business on East Washington Street at the end of 1908, he became the sales agent in Athens for Curtiss Motorcycles. The Curtiss Motorcycle Company had been established by Glenn Hammond Curtiss of Hammondsport, New York. The company had been building "Hercules" motorcycles in Hammond-sport since 1902.

Curtiss was a long-time speed enthusiast. In January 1907, at Ormond Beach, Florida, he was officially clocked riding his motorcycle at a speed of 136.3 miles per hour, earning him the moniker "Fastest Man on Earth," a title he carried for years. That same year Curtiss started his aviation career. It was a career that would establish Curtiss as the founder of the American Aircraft Industry and Father of Naval Aviation.[21]

Also in 1907, Curtiss joined the Aerial Experiment Association (the "A.E.A."), a group of individuals that included Alexander Graham Bell, which was building pusher-type biplanes. On 12 March 1908, at Keuka Lake, New York, the group's first plane, the A.E.A. "Red Wing," made the first public flight in the United States of a heavier-than-air machine. Although the Wright brothers were the first to fly, their initial flight was not open to the public or the press (the Wrights had a distrust of the press and preferred to conduct their work in secret). The A.E.A. "Red Wing" flew for twenty seconds, covering a distance of just under 319 feet before crashing.[22]

Although Curtiss was not piloting the A.E.A. "Red Wing" when it made its initial flight, he was at the controls of the group's second airplane, the A.E.A. "White Wing," two months later for its first flight. Another pusher-type biplane, the "White Wing" flew 1,017 feet. Curtiss also piloted the group's third plane, the A.E.A. "June Bug," yet another pusher-type biplane, on its initial flight on 4 July 1908, across Pleasant Valley, New York, for a distance of 5,090 feet (almost one mile), achieving the first officially recognized, pre-announced, and publicly observed flight in the United States.[23]

Some five months after achieving his latest record, Curtiss traveled to Athens to meet with Ben and check on his Curtiss Motorcycle sales agency. It was on this trip that Curtiss learned that Ben and Zumpt were attempting to build an airplane of their own. Fresh on the heels of the success that the A.E.A. was enjoying in its aviation pursuit, Curtiss recommended that the proposed Epps-Huff biplane design follow the pusher-type design that the A.E.A. was using.[24] Curtiss's suggestion was the only time the Epps-Huff partnership accepted input from an aviation professional, and on this occasion the only help they received was the suggestion that the propeller face aft.

Assembling the wheel undercarriage to the Epps-Huff I was a relatively quick and simple process, after which Ben and Zumpt were ready to test their ability to control the plane in flight. Like the Wrights' and the A.E.A.'s airplanes, the Epps-Huff I utilized wing warping to maintain control in flight. With no prior experience, the wing warping technique was a skill that had to be self-taught, and the only way to learn was by trial and error. Ben and Zumpt decided that the best way to master this technique was to test their biplane as glider, before a heavy engine was installed.

Many decades later, Zumpt related to a granddaughter and her husband that one of the first attempts to test the Epps-Huff I as a glider took place at night. Before attracting too much public attention, they wanted to make sure their biplane could be controlled and flown successfully. They decided to conduct a test under the cover of darkness, away from public scrutiny. In the middle of the night, when the streets of Athens were deserted of pedestrian traffic, they loaded the biplane onto a horse-drawn dray and hauled the plane from the East Washington Street garage to the old fairgrounds on Chase Street, the former location of the Northeast Georgia Fair.

The fairgrounds consisted of forty acres, which were purchased in 1903, on the northeast edge of the city. It was located on the main line of the Seaboard Air Line, one block from the line of the Athens Street Railway Company. The site consisted of a one-half mile horse track and a grandstand with seating capacity for 2,200 people. It was praised as "one of the finest half-mile tracks in the entire South." Some eighty stables were built for the racehorses along the fence on the Chase Street side of the grounds. During fair week there were pacer, trotter, and runner horse races of various furlong lengths and the featured one-mile Athens Derby race.[25]

Ben and Zumpt were anxious to get their biplane in the air in order to test its wing warping capabilities and to gain experience themselves in controlling it in flight. They launched the glider from a hill near the racetrack. For a first attempt Ben and Zumpt were pleased with the glider's performance, but it made a rather hard landing. It hit the ground close to the pen on the infield of the racetrack where the county's work mules were boarded. The impact was so sudden and loud that it spooked the mules. The startled mules broke out of their pen and scattered across the fairgrounds.

There was no way Ben and Zumpt could round up all the mules and get them back into the pen, so in a state of panic, they did the only thing they could think of: they gathered up everything they'd brought to the racetrack and quickly hauled their biplane on the dray back to the garage before anyone caught them.

The next day, word quickly spread around town that the county mules had broken out of their pen during the night and that it had taken hours for the sheriff's deputies to find them all and get them back into the pen. There was a lot a speculation about what might have caused the mules to be spooked, but none of the speculation centered on Ben, Zumpt, or their biplane, so their antics of that night were never discovered.[26]

After the incident with the county mules, there were no more nighttime tests of the Epps-Huff I. Instead, Ben and Zumpt returned to the racetrack to conduct further tests in daylight. These tests continued with the biplane being used as a glider. They found that the best way to conduct tests of the wing-warping component of the biplane and to hone their piloting skills was by tying a towrope to the biplane and pulling it around the racetrack. They used a Studebaker-E.M.F 30 chassis with the Demi Tonneau body removed to pull the biplane. The E.M.F. 30 was an automobile manufactured by Studebaker-E.M.F. in Detroit. In 1909, this company was the fourth largest automobile manufacturer in the United States. The Demi Tonneau had a convertible-style body, one of four body styles available for this 30-horsepower automobile.[27] Ben and Zumpt switched off between driving and piloting the biplane so that each was able to offer input into improving its performance.[28]

Unfortunately, the Epps-Huff I had a short life. After several weeks of testing at the racetrack, the towrope broke and the biplane crashed into the ground, reducing it to little more than a pile of splintered wood, snapped cables, and torn fabric. It would have to be totally rebuilt. But Ben and Zumpt had learned a lot from this experience. They believed their two fixed-wing design was too rigid for the wing warping technique to control the biplane successfully.

As summer was getting underway and work on their dream of flying continued, a new military company was organized in Athens as part of the state militia. This company was named the "Clarke Rifles" and designated as Company F of the Third Battalion. Ben and Zumpt, along with fifty-nine other young men in Athens, signed up and participated in drills that were held several times a week.[29] The exercise and time away from airplane building helped clear their minds and give them a refreshed perspective on how to proceed with their dream. It didn't take long for Ben to come up with an idea.

Ben suggested a new, completely different design. Instead of a biplane, their next design would be a monoplane, a single fixed-wing design. According to Zumpt, neither he nor Ben had seen a photograph or a drawing of a monoplane, but that was not a deterrent. They'd read that several other aviators were experimenting with monoplane designs, which seemed to be the design of the future. Ben went to work on his design concept for a monoplane. But before the newly designed monoplane could fly, they would need an engine.

3

The Search for an Airplane Engine

Ben and Zumpt began looking for an engine while they were building the Epps-Huff I. They were aware that weight was a critical factor in getting their plane off the ground. Most automobiles at that time were powered by a water-cooled gasoline engine. These engines, like today's modern internal combustion engines, were cooled by a closed circuit carrying a liquid coolant. The coolant traveled through channels in the engine block, absorbing heat as it went, to a radiator, where the coolant released the heat into the air. These engines are referred to as "water-cooled" because they utilize a liquid-coolant circuit. These engines are very heavy.

Instead of a water-cooled engine, Ben wanted to use an air-cooled engine, which had the advantage of being a much lighter-weight engine. In contrast to a liquid-coolant circuit, an air-cooled engine releases heat directly into the air. This is generally done with metal fins covering the outside of the cylinders, which increase the surface area on which air can act. Motorcycles use air-cooled engines for the benefits of weight reduction and less complexity.

In 1909, the largest manufacturer of gasoline engines in the United States was Ford Motor Company. All of the automobile engines built by Ford were the heavy, water-cooled ones. But with their knowledge, expertise, manufacturing facilities, and financial resources, Ben and Zumpt didn't see any reason why Ford Motor Company couldn't build the best air-cooled gasoline engine in the world. With the boldness of youth, Ben and Zumpt wrote to Henry Ford, the great American industrialist and arguably the most influential American inventor of the twentieth century. In the letter they sent to Dearborn, Michigan, they described their project of building a monoplane and asked whether Ford Motor Company would build an air-cooled gasoline engine to power their monoplane.

Henry Ford himself sent the company's short reply in a personally signed letter: "Ford Motor Company does not wish to become involved in airplanes."[1] That was the end of the Epps-Huff partnership's proposed business venture with Ford Motor Company. There was no further communication. The story ended with Henry Ford's pithy response, as far as Ben and Zumpt knew, but in Michigan there was more to the story.

Some time after replying to the letter from Ben and Zumpt, Henry Ford summoned to his office his fifteen-year-old son, Edsel. He told Edsel he was going to provide him and Edsel's friend, Charles Van Auken, with three Ford factory workers and directed Edsel to undertake the project of building a monoplane. Young Edsel and his crew went to work designing and building the first Ford Motor Company airplane.

The Ford monoplane featured wing warping controls and a tricycle gear, like Ben and Zumpt's plane and was powered by a Ford Model T engine. The Ford Motor Company had started manufacturing Model T automobiles in September 1908. The engine in the Model T had four cylinders that produced 20-horsepower and a top speed for the Model T of forty-five miles per hour. Unlike the configuration of the radiator with the engine in the Ford Model T automobile, the radiator for the Ford plane engine was angled perpendicular to the wind in order to reduce air resistance.

The Ford plane made multiple test flights from the Fort Wayne parade grounds in 1910, but never flew well.[2] The plane's last attempt at flight ended in a crash into a tree, and the project was scrapped.

It is not known how much detail of their plane's design Ben and Zumpt furnished to Henry Ford in their letter request, and there is no evidence this letter influenced Henry Ford or Edsel in the decision to build or in the design of the Ford plane, but it was quite coincidental that Henry Ford had his son build a monoplane shortly after receiving a letter request from two young men in Athens. It's a coincidence that is hard to dismiss.

Undaunted by Henry Ford's rejection, Ben and Zumpt turned to another source for their engine, which involved two more world-renowned personalities. Ben and Zumpt set their sights on finding a suitable lightweight motorcycle engine, but it had to be an engine that could generate the power they needed to get their plane into the air. They contacted Palmer Walthour of Walthour & Hood, a bicycle shop in Atlanta.[3] Palmer had in his shop exactly what Ben and Zumpt needed: it was a used motorcycle with an Anzani two-cylinder engine that was owned by perhaps the greatest athlete in the world at the time.

Palmer Walthour was an older brother of the world-famous cyclist Bobby Walthour (Robert Howe Walthour, Sr.). In the 1890s and early 1900s, competitive cycling was one of the top sports in the United States. The three most common types of bicycle races were sprints, six-day races, and motor-paced racing. Bobby excelled in all three, but started out as a sprinter. He first appeared in the Atlanta papers as an amateur cyclist in 1895. A short time later he turned professional and quickly became a superstar. It was in motor-paced racing that Bobby reached superstar status.[4]

Motor-paced competition involved bicycles racing around an oval track made of wood with steeply banked turns. The bicycles were tucked inches behind a pacing motorcycle traveling at speeds greater than fifty miles per hour. The sport had its origin in England in 1895 and migrated to the northern United States, where Bobby Walthour was introduced to it in 1899. Bobby brought the sport south in fall 1899 with his first race in the Piedmont Coliseum at Piedmont Park in Atlanta.[5]

The sport drew tremendous crowds, which sat awestruck from the nonstop action and loud noise. The crowds were addicted to the dangers the riders faced. It was the most violent and deadly sport in the modern era.[6] The bicyclists did not wear helmets, protective clothing, or any other type of protection as they pedaled, tucking mere inches behind a pacing motorcycle in the slipstream. The slipstream was the area where the airstream created reduced air pressure and forward suction directly behind the rapidly moving motorcycle. The bicycle that Bobby raced was a fixed-gear safety, which did not include brakes. Instead, he used his legs to work against the inertia of the forward-moving pedals or hopped off and ran along the side of the bicycle.[7]

It didn't take Bobby long to dominate the sport. He was the United States national champion in 1902 and 1903 and was the world professional bicycle champion in 1904 and 1905.[8] He was treated like a king in Europe and was just as popular in the United States. He made fabulous money from his sport, more than any other professional athlete in his generation. In Georgia, it was said that "for many years, the only athletes to achieve greatness from Georgia were Ty Cobb, Bobby Jones and Bobby Walthour. And…everyone in Atlanta knew when you talked about 'Bobby,' it was Walthour not Jones."[9]

Bobby, along with his brother, Palmer, came to Athens in fall 1903 for an exhibition race at the Northeast Georgia Fair.[10] The fair started on 5 October 1903, and opening day was designated as "Bobby Walthour Day." Bobby was billed as "the fastest bicycle rider in the world" and he was scheduled to ride at the racetrack against five of the fastest horses in Georgia in a five-mile relay race. Bobby was to ride the five miles straight through while a fresh horse would be started at the end of each mile.[11] Before a packed grandstand, which included Governor J. M. Terrell, the guest of honor, Bobby easily won and collected his winnings.

On the day that Bobby raced at the fairgrounds in Athens, Ben would have been in Atlanta attending classes at Georgia Tech. Zumpt had reunited with his siblings, father, and new stepmother that summer, but had not yet moved to Athens. There is no evidence that

Zumpt attended the Northeast Georgia Fair on Bobby Walthour Day, but Zumpt was living in Northeast Georgia and the fair was heavily advertised throughout the region. With the fame that Bobby Walthour had in Georgia, there can be no doubt that both Ben and Zumpt would have been aware that he was racing in Athens.

In order to maintain a sharp, competitive edge Bobby had to invest in and keep up with the latest developments in motorcycle technology. In 1905 there was one person in particular who was making the most significant contributions to this technology and whose accomplishments were catching the eye of the European press. That person was twenty-seven-year-old Alessandro Anzani.

Anzani was born near Milan, Italy, in 1877, and at an early age showed a passionate and talented disposition for mechanics. He was a fanatic about cycling and developed into a good, competitive cyclist. While attending a rally in Milan as a spectator, he met and over time became good friends with the French cyclist Gabriel Poulain, who would become the world sprint champion in 1905 and second in the world in 1906 and 1908. In 1900, at Poulain's urging, Anzani immigrated to France to take part in bicycle racing.[12]

Anzani lived with Poulain in France, where he met an amateur engineer by the name of Cornet from Marseilles, who was building motorcycles in a small workshop. During conversations, Anzani told Cornet of his passion for mechanics, especially motorcycle engines. Cornet offered him a small workshop where he could work in his spare time to develop a motorcycle engine of his own. Anzani abandoned bicycle racing and accepted the offer. Cornet assigned Anzani the task of building a two-cylinder engine that would be lighter in weight and more powerful than any other engine of its class at the time.[13]

Anzani developed his engine and mounted it on a motorcycle frame. He raced the motorcycle himself and had immediate success, winning numerous races. His new engine proved to be lighter and more powerful than any other two-cylinder engine at the time. In

1905, Anzani established a world record of 100 kilometers per hour for an engine of its class. He used the money that he won from motorcycle racing to set up his own small workshop at Asnières, near Paris, where he built the most powerful lightweight, two-cylinder motorcycle engines in the world.[14]

After winning the 1905 motor-paced world championship, Bobby Walthour remained in Europe to race the German champion, Thaddeus Robl, at the Velodrome in Paris that November. During his stay in France, Bobby heard about the success Anzani was having with his engines and the reputation he was building as the best. Always wanting to keep on the cutting edge in the technology of his sport, Bobby arranged to buy two pacer motorcycles from Anzani equipped with the two-cylinder engine he'd developed. Bobby had his pacer, Gussie Lawson, considered the best pacer in the world and known as the "Terrible Swede," ride the new pacers while preparing for his race in Paris. Bobby and Gussie were ecstatic over the new pacers as Gussie was able to power these machines up to sixty miles per hour during Bobby's training sessions.[15]

Riding behind his new motor-pacers, powered by the Anzani twin-cylinder engines, Walthour beat Robl in all three races in the Velodrome and set several track records.[16]

Bobby, his family, and Gussie Lawson boarded a steamer for New York in late November, bringing the new motorcycles with Anzani engines with him. He planned to ride in the Madison Square Garden six-day race scheduled to begin on 4 December 1905, but was unable to find a partner to his liking and dropped out. However, he did perform exhibitions for the crowd in Madison Square Garden during the six-day race, and he rode these exhibitions behind Gussie, who showed off the new motor-pacers with the Anzani engines to the delight of the crowd. When the six-day race concluded, Bobby returned to Atlanta, bringing his new motor-pacers with him.[17]

While Ben and Zumpt were busy building their first airplane at the start of 1909, Bobby was at his Atlanta home at 28 Peachtree

Place,[18] preparing for the upcoming European racing season. He and Gussie Lawson crossed the Atlantic in late April to race in France.[19] Left behind in his brother, Palmer's, bicycle shop was at least one of the Anzani twin-cylinder pacer-motorcycles that Bobby had acquired in Paris four years earlier.

As summer approached, Ben and Zumpt saw the Anzani engine in Palmer's shop on South Forsyth Street and knew it was exactly what they needed. It was a lightweight, air-cooled engine with a reputation for outstanding performance. A deal was reached with Palmer to purchase one of the Anzani motor-pacers: Ben traded Palmer an older model, two-seat Cadillac automobile for the pacer and hauled it back to the garage on East Washington Street.[20]

At the time, neither Ben nor Zumpt knew that they would hear the name "Anzani" again a few short months later. Anzani was teaming up with a pioneer aviator who would have a direct influence on the work of the Epps-Huff partnership. But for now, Ben and Zumpt had their engine and they were ready to install it in their newly designed plane, the second design for the Epps-Huff partnership. It was the Epps-Huff II, their first attempt at a monoplane.

4

The First Epps-Huff Monoplane

After the Epps-Huff I Biplane wrecked as a result of the broken towrope, Ben decided to build a monoplane. He and Zumpt learned from their biplane that wing warping did not provide enough flexibility to control flight when it was used with the two fixed-wings design. Flexing structural members made control difficult and tended to cause structural failure. There was more flexibility when the wing warping technique was used in a single fixed-wing design. Although monoplanes were more amenable to wing warping, the prevailing view at the time was that monoplanes were more unstable and more dangerous. It was difficult to master the wing warping technique flying a monoplane due to the tendency to overcorrect.

According to Zumpt, Ben had not seen a monoplane before he began designing his concept of what a monoplane should look like.[1] They used parts from the Epps-Huff I that were salvageable, and by early summer 1909, construction of the new monoplane, the Epps-Huff II, was complete with the two-cylinder Anzani engine installed. As they'd done with the Epps-Huff I, Ben and Zumpt moved the Epps-Huff II out of the garage onto the clay street to be photographed.

This time the photograph shows a boyish-looking Ben dressed in a buttoned, short-collar suit jacket and pants, wearing what appears to be the same newsboy cap that he wore in the earlier photograph with the biplane. He's standing next to the Epps-Huff II Monoplane with Epps Garage in the background (Image Number 6).

This photograph is by far the most reproduced photograph of all those in Ben's scrapbook. It is the quintessential photograph associated with the beginning of aviation in Georgia. This photo accompanies many of the articles written over the decades about the first airplane flight in Georgia, but most of the reprints are cropped at the bottom so that an interesting notation written on the original photograph does not appear.

The original photograph has a handwritten note, in blue pen near the bottom, that reads, "One of the First Built 1907 - 2 cylinder Anzani motor." This notation closely resembles Ben's handwriting and is presumed to have been written by Ben. The notation is correct with one glaring exception, the date: *1907*.

It is not known when this notation was written on the photo-graph. The photograph was first published in a newspaper, the *Athens Banner-Herald*, in 1929. The caption under the photograph in that issue states that this plane "was built by Ben Epps in his garage back in 1909."[2] It is hard to imagine that the newspaper caption would have used the date 1909 if the handwritten notation with the date 1907 was on the original photograph at that time.

Eleven months later, this quintessential photograph accompa-nied an article in the *Atlanta Constitution Magazine.* Inexplicably, the caption under the photograph in this publication stated, "Mr. Epps made the plane in his shops during 1907."[3]

The Epps-Huff II Monoplane was not built in 1907. As previously noted, Ben did not have his garage at 120 East Washington Street, where this plane and the Epps-Huff I were built, until late November or December 1908. In addition to the quintessential photograph, there are two other photographs that are known to exist of the Epps-Huff II on East Washington Street in front of Epps Garage. These two photographs are reproduced as Images Numbers 7 and 8 herein. The original photograph of Image Number 7 is in Ben's scrapbook and also has the date "1907" written in blue pen on the white border at the bottom. The location of the original photograph of Image Number 8 is unknown. Image Number

8 was reproduced from a copy in the collection of Gary L. Doster, which he obtained from Ben Epps, Jr., in 1997.

There is no way of knowing when Image Numbers 7 and 8 were taken in relation to when the quintessential photograph was taken. All three photographs are of the same plane, the Epps-Huff II Monoplane, with the single difference being that a fuel tank has been placed on top of the wing in Image Numbers 7 and 8 that is not on the wing in the quintessential photograph (Image Number 6).

The quintessential photograph was taken with the camera lens showing Washington Street as it proceeds west. In the other two photographs, the camera lens is pointed to the east as Washington Street inclines to its intersection with College Avenue. In Image Number 7 the tall building in the background on the right (south) side of Washington Street, which fronts on College Avenue, is the former Southern Mutual Building. Construction of this building was not finished until summer 1908.[4] In Image Number 8 the tall building in the background on the left (north) side of Washington Street, immediately past the intersection with College Avenue, which has a light-colored, sandstone band under the top floor windows, is the former Georgian Hotel. This lot is where Washington Street School was formerly located. The school building was torn down so that this hotel could be constructed, but the Georgian Hotel did not open until 1 March 1909,[5] which means these two photographs could not have been taken any earlier than 1909, despite the fact of the "1907" notation.

Zumpt also confirmed that the notation "1907" on the quintessential photograph was not correct. Zumpt had a copy of the quintessential photograph made in 1970 for his scrapbook. On his copy, Zumpt used a pen to change Ben's handwritten "7" into a "9" to reflect that the date was 1909, not 1907. Zumpt also typed on his copy of this photograph, "This monoplane plane [the Epps-Huff II] was constructed from the parts of our original Bi-plane [sic], after it was partially damaged while toweing [sic] it around the racetrack....

The notation made on [this photograph] that this plane was flown by Ben in 1907 is without foundation and by some one who was overe [*sic*] enthused, or what ever was the idea is not correct."[6]

With the publication of the quintessential photograph in the *Atlanta Constitution* in 1930 and the accompanying caption, the narrative of when the Epps-Huff II was constructed changed. Every article appearing after that publication, which proffered the year of the construction of the Epps-Huff II, stated that it was 1907.

Despite the mistake in the notation as to the year of construction, these photographs nevertheless depict important details of the construction of the Epps-Huff II. It was a distinctly different design from what the Epps-Huff partnership had built previously. The photographs of the Epps-Huff II on East Washington Street show that the propeller and Anzani engine had been installed. The propeller was approximately six feet in length and positioned behind the wing. Again, the new design followed the recommendation of Glenn Curtiss that they build a pusher-type configuration; the propeller faced aft.

Designed as a monoplane, the Epps-Huff II had a single, elongated fixed-wing with a 35-foot span and a chord length, being the distance from the leading edge to the trialing edge of the wing, of eight feet. The wing was angled up to improve lift. There was a single support beam the length of the span, running along the center of the wing. This beam, known as the main spar, was the central structural member of the wing.

The main spar was attached to and crossed, at a perpendicular angle, a series of evenly spaced wooden ribs running the length of the chord. The ribs also shared in carrying the load of the wing. A cloth fabric skin, again made on Ben's mother's sewing machine, was stretched across the underside of the wing's ribs. The wing was further supported with cable wires that were attached to the top of the wing and connected to vertical supporting posts. A significantly taller vertical post on the leading edge of the wing, the king post, was centered on the span. A shorter vertical post was centered on the span at the trailing edge of the wing. Cables were also used to attach the wing to the undercarriage frame.

The plane was guided to the right or left by a large, flat, vertical rudder positioned ten feet behind the wing. Like the wing, the rudder was skinned with cloth fabric. Positioned about six feet in front of the wing was a double-plane elevator, a canard wing shaped like a box kite, only larger. The elevator frame was three feet by eight feet, with both the top and bottom horizontal planes skinned in fabric. The elevator could be tilted up or down in order to lift or descend the plane. Both the rudder and elevator were controlled from the pilot's seat. The plane was also designed for the pilot to use wing warping to control the flight.

The undercarriage of the monoplane consisted of three bicycle wheels in a triangle formation, with one wheel at the leading edge of the wing and the other two at the trailing edge. There was a single wagon bench under the wing, where the pilot sat upright, midway between the front wheel and the back two wheels. By contrast, Orville Wright did not sit up, but rather lay flat to pilot the 1903 Wright Flyer. In addition, the body of the Wright Flyer was not supported on wheels. It took off from a rail.

As completed, the Epps-Huff II Monoplane had a heavy, unwieldy appearance and seemed unlikely to achieve flight. To get a feel for how their new design would handle, Ben and Zumpt decided to test it on Washington Street. The street in front of the garage was nothing more than red clay, but it was becoming one of the leading business streets in Athens. The Colonial Opera House was located on this street. The street passed the side of the Federal Building, which housed the post office and federal court, and also passed the side of city hall. An editorial in the *Athens Weekly Banner* called on the city council to make the paving of Washington Street the first street improvement for 1907.[7] However, this section of Washington Street remained clay until it was finally paved in brick in 1917.[8]

As one of the most heavily traveled streets in Athens, when it rained, wagon wheels cut deep trenches into the clay. Residents often complained, probably with some exaggeration, that after several days of heavy rain, the mud on Washington Street could be "more than knee deep."[9] After Washington Street dried from the spring rains in 1909, the Epps-Huff II Monoplane was hauled out of the garage to be tested.

The section of Washington Street used for the test ran from the base of the Confederate Monument,[10] a tall Italian marble monolith in the middle of the intersection with College Avenue, being the peak elevation of Washington Street, and descended down to Pulaski Street. This stretch of Washington Street was three blocks in length. Ben and Zumpt took turns piloting the plane and studying its reaction to the controls; while one was in the pilot's seat, the other observed the plane's performance to pinpoint improvements that could be made to enhance its capability.

In 1970, Zumpt recalled what it was like to test the Epps-Huff II Monoplane on Washington Street:

> We Rode [sic] this plane up and down Washington Street from in front of the garage, to the intersection of College Avenue. Here we began to learn the problems of turning an areoplane around once [sic] turned we would head down West [sic] on Washington Street too [sic] Pulaski here we faced our problem again turning, it rode on bicycle wheels, [sic] We were taught how fragile a bicycle wheel was when out of its forks onto an airplane. Up and down Washington Street we would ride the plane makeing [sic] improvements Ben deemed necessary to it [sic] perfect operation. He did get it to skim off the ground, each had his turn while the other observed, trying to fathom our trouble. It would not rise over a foot or two from the ground, the motor either conked out or starting [sic] to slow down.[11]

The above narrative was typed by Zumpt on the back of his copy of the quintessential picture of the Epps-Huff II Monoplane. This narrative was one of several that Zumpt typed in 1970 on notecards and on photographs he possessed of some of the planes built by the Epps-Huff partnership. At the time Zumpt typed these narratives, he was eighty years old. Other than the photographs, he had no reference materials of any kind to help refresh his memory. Despite these limiting circumstances, Zumpt's narratives display a remarkably detailed recollection of events that occurred more than sixty years in his past.

Zumpt referred to this monoplane as the "guinea pig."[12] It never performed in the manner they wanted; however, it did make significant contributions to the Epps-Huff partnership's pursuit of flight and was considered a great learning experience. Zumpt wrote,

> This plane taught us many things we were unable to disgest [sic] their full meaning at the time...such as finding out you could turn the plane, by holding down a left or right corner of the wing, we [sic] were not able to understand the full meaning of this discover [sic] by us until late in 1909, we devoted more time to it in the early part of 1910. It was what others discovered and called "it the aileron." [sic]...we found the propellor [sic] had to have certain pitches, and this had to be in tolerance with the horsepower of the engine.... We found our propeller had to be of a stabilized pitch, a precise and smooth depth, with a feather edge, cutting into the air was its main function, the depth it cut was dependent on the horsepower of our Engine [sic].[13]

Despite adjustments made to the monoplane, after repeated trials on Washington Street it became clear that the Epps-Huff II was not capable of sustained, controlled flight. Their "guinea pig" proved too heavy, too unstable, and too unwieldy for a successful flight. Zumpt acknowledged, "This plane was never flown by Ben or myself. It was however a great experiment for us."[14]

The Epps-Huff II Monoplane never achieved a level of performance for Ben and Zumpt to deem it worthy enough to take to the field in Athens that they had selected as the best place to attempt the first flight. After many unsuccessful attempts to improve it, Ben and

Zumpt decided to abandon this model.[15] Their solution was to reconfigure the plane.

The Epps-Huff II was disassembled and work immediately began on building the Epps-Huff III. This model was also a monoplane and had the same look as their first monoplane. However, this model was smaller, lighter, better balanced, and more stable. The wingspan of the second monoplane was shortened and the chord length reduced. The single, main spar running down the center of the wing was replaced with two spars running span-wise for more strength. The front spar was approximately one-quarter of the chord length from the leading edge of the wing, and the second spar parallel to the first, about a quarter of the chord length from the aft edge.

More wire was added to the top of the wing for better bracing. But instead of relying exclusively on wire braces to support the load of the wing, a strut was attached to the underside of the wing on each side of the fuselage and anchored into the undercarriage. By providing outward-facing support, these structural components acted to resist longitudinal compression of the wing at its tips. This enabled the struts to keep the wing from sagging at its tips as the plane attempted to lift into the air, which would inhibit the monoplane's ability to lift off the ground.

As was done with the Epps-Huff II, the wing had a series of wood ribs attached to the spars running down the span of the wing, perpendicular to the spars. Stretched-cloth skin was attached to the underside of the spars and ribs to share the load. The skinned double-plane elevator was positioned in front of the wing and the skinned flat-plane rudder was at the rear of the plane, as was done with their first monoplane. But the distance of the rudder from the frame was shortened and the frame reconfigured to better accommodate the propeller. The same 15-horsepower Anzani engine was installed to power the Epps-Huff III Monoplane.

Ben and Zumpt spent many weeknights and weekend hours in the garage, during late July and August, getting their new plane ready.

They'd been hard at work for almost nine months on their dream of a successful flight. To this point, they had nothing to show for their exhaustive effort. But to them, failure was not falling down, failure was not getting back up. Others might have given up the quest by this time, but not Ben and Zumpt; they doggedly clung to their optimism. As they worked on the Epps-Huff III Monoplane, they were as confident as ever their dream would be achieved. This lighter, sleeker, and more stable model was going to fly.

The location where Ben and Zumpt would make their first attempt at a sustained, controlled flight had been selected at the beginning of their quest for flight. It was an open area within the city limit, a few blocks beyond Ben's parents's home on West Hancock Avenue.

As August was drawing to a close, construction of the Epps-Huff III Monoplane was complete. This model was worthy of more than a trial on Washington Street; this one would be tested in the open field.

The citizens of Athens had been waiting since May to see an airplane fly. That was when they first read in the *Athens Banner* that the Epps-Huff partnership was building the first airplane in Georgia. Summer had come and was almost gone. Everyone was anxious to see what the new model looked like and clamoring for Ben and Zumpt to set a date for their first field trial. The trial date had to be a day that didn't interfere with Ben's or Zumpt's day jobs or with church services, so it was determined that a Saturday would be the best day. A date was set and word began to spread, creating more excitement in Athens than when the great Bobby Walthour had come to town to race at the fair.

A large crowd of spectators was sure to be present. Newspaper reporters and most likely photographers would also be on hand. Ben and Zumpt's success or failure would be published in papers across the state. They didn't want to disappoint. As the date approached, anxious anticipation drove fluttering stomach butterflies to a fevered pitch. This would be their first attempt at flight in an open field, a much more daunting task than traveling a couple hundred feet at a slow pace up and down Washington Street. Neither Ben nor Zumpt would get any sleep the night before.

28 August 1909
Lynwood Park, Athens, Georgia

The sun was cresting the horizon on the Saturday that the Epps-Huff III Monoplane was loaded on a horse-drawn dray in front of the garage on East Washington Street. Ben and Zumpt were getting an early start to avoid the humidity and heat that would set in by noon, pushing the temperature to the mid-90s. The day was forecast to be the hottest of the year so far. But more importantly, the early start would ensure that the test flight was conducted in still air, before the rising temperature kicked up winds that could affect the control of the plane.

With a crowd of spectators following behind, the procession slowly plodded out West Hancock Avenue, past Ben's parents's home, and turned on Billups Street, heading to the entrance of Lynwood Park. The park, an extension of the Cobbham District, had been platted for residential development in 1906.[1] According to the recorded plat, Lynwood Park was a long, rectangular-shaped parcel, west of the downtown area. The southeast corner of the park began at the intersection of West Hancock Avenue and Billups Street. The park was bounded by the following streets: Cobb Street on the north, Billups Street on the east, Hancock Avenue on the south, and Hillcrest Avenue on the west. According to the 1906 plat, the park was to be traversed through the center by a wide, two-lane road with the lanes separated by a traffic island; this road was named The Plaza. But in August 1909, The Plaza had not been built, nor had any residential development taken place; the park was largely an open field with terracing. At the end of The Plaza, near the western boundary of the park where two creeks merge, a lake was proposed to be built ("Phinizy Lake").[2]

Lynwood Park was three blocks west of Milledge Avenue. It had an excellent site at the top of a hill, where Hill Street was located, to launch an airplane. From Hill Street, the park was a continuous downward slope over open land to its southern boundary.

With the help of friends, Ben and Zumpt unloaded the dray and made the final assembly of their monoplane at the top of the hill. After the assembly was complete, the monoplane was rolled into position, facing southwest. After a final check, Ben climbed into the pilot's seat. It was time to start the engine.

The fuel tank on top of the wing had been topped off before leaving the East Washington Street garage. The engine would run on naphtha instead of gasoline. Similar to gasoline, naphtha is the volatile fraction of liquid hydrocarbons in petroleum. It's a colorless to reddish-brown aromatic liquid sometimes referred to as "white gas." The use of naphtha was another of the partnership's money-saving measures. Gasoline cost 10 cents a gallon in 1909, but Ben and Zumpt were able to purchase naphtha for only 8 cents a gallon.[3] They used the less expensive fuel despite the fact that it was more flammable than gasoline. Ben and Zumpt were well aware that if the plane crashed, Ben would have to instantly shut the engine off, jump out, and scramble away as quickly as possible to avoid a probable fiery explosion.

By the time Ben and Zumpt arrived at Lynwood Park with their plane in tow, a crowd was already present. The spectators buzzed with comments on the look of the Epps-Huff III and speculation as to whether it would fly. People were positioning to get the best view possible. They lined the sides of the field along the projected flight path.[4] Some were crossing in front of the plane to meet friends or just to be on the other side. One person in particular was making sure he had a clear view of the first attempt at flight: he was a newspaper reporter and had his notepad in hand.

Ben, wearing his newsboy cap and seated on the old wagon bench, positioned his hands and feet on the plane's control devices. Zumpt, wearing a white shirt with the sleeves cut short and his black derby cocked at a slight angle, moved to the front of the plane after making sure Ben was positioned as comfortable as possible and ready to start the engine. Zumpt grabbed the propeller with both hands and, with Ben's nod, he pulled down hard to crank the engine. The propeller began to spin and the Anzani motor spit a dingy cloud of exhaust from the engine.

Zumpt held on to his derby with one hand and signaled, one thumb up, with his other, before moving to the rear of the plane to watch. Ben revved the engine in preparation to take off. Those standing nearby covered their ears from the painful, deafening noise. As the plane began to inch forward, fingers crossed and prayers were said. The plane picked up speed, although its forward movement was anything but smooth as a result of the uneven ground.

The reporter fervently made notes as he watched,

> The monoplane got a bad start, but succeeded in clearing the ground by about 1 foot and skimmed through the air above the ground for 50 yards. The machine bumped into a terrace, and it was all over. The machine was not badly damaged, and all the damages were repaired in a few hours. Another trial of the machine will be made Monday morning.[5]

The headline and the first sentence of the article in Monday's edition of the *Atlanta Constitution* said it all: "Flight Is Made By Georgia Man," "Athens claims the first aeroplane flight in the state of Georgia."[6]

Zumpt had watched the flight from the top of the hill. The monoplane lifted slightly into the air and Ben was able to keep it airborne and under control for a brief period of time. It cleared the first terrace but then veered to the right and butted into a barbed-wire fence at the second terrace and crashed.[7]

As soon as the plane struck the ground, Ben cut the engine and jumped clear. Zumpt sprinted down the hill to check on Ben. The crowd was also converging around Ben and the plane. When Zumpt was sure Ben was okay, he was able to breathe again. Then the reality that the Epps-Huff III had flown hit home. A grin spread across Zumpt's face.

With some difficulty, Zumpt pushed through the crowd to reach the plane. He did a quick assessment and deemed the damage readily repairable. He rejoined Ben and together they found themselves at the center of a tightly packed, cheering crowd.

The wildly excited spectators heaped praise on Ben and Zumpt and jockeyed for position to shake their hands and pat them on the back. The reporter also made his way to the center of the crowd, where he added his congratulations and sought reactions from the young aviators. In his article about the flight, he reported,

> The two young men...were well satisfied in getting the machine to clear the ground even for a small distance.... Quite a crowd will witness the second trial of the Machine [on Monday].[8]

The Epps-Huff III Monoplane traveled a distance of 150 feet on its first attempt. The Epps-Huff partnership beat the Wright brothers' initial distance of 120 feet on the world's first successful flight. The Wright brothers' first flight in December 1903 was in a biplane. The world's first successful flight by a monoplane did not occur until April 1907. Frenchman Louis Blériot is credited with flying the world's first successful monoplane, and his record-setting flight took place in France, where his Blériot V Monoplane covered a distance of only twenty feet, after a 305-foot run.[9]

Fewer than thirty months after the first successful flight of a monoplane in the *world*, two young men from Athens, Georgia, (Ben was twenty-one and Zumpt a teenager for one more month) built and flew their own version of a monoplane. The Epps-Huff partnership's monoplane flew a distance that was seven-and-a-half-times farther than the Blériot V had achieved.

Their feat was nothing short of miraculous. Neither Ben nor Zumpt had any formal education or training in airplane design or aerodynamics. Except for Glenn Curtiss's suggestion that they build a pusher-type plane, they received no third-party help. They relied on trade journals, their own imaginations, and their God-given talents, along with their character for tenacious perseverance. Their entire enterprise was financed solely from their own meager incomes.

On Monday morning, 30 August 1909, newspapers across the state carried headlines of the historic event that had occurred over the weekend in Athens. The *Atlanta Georgian & News* proclaimed, "Georgians Make Flight in a New Aeroplane, Athens Young Men Skim Over Earth in Newly Constructed Aerial Craft in Which They Hope to Rival Noted Aeronauts."[10] In Augusta the local paper told its readers that "Two Athens Boys Invent Aeroplane."[11] Georgians in Savannah woke up on Monday to read, "Short Flight of Georgia Monoplane, Young Men at Athens Meet Ground with a Bump."[12] The names "Ben Epps" and "Zumpt Huff" also appeared in the Macon paper as a result of their historic Saturday achievement. The *Macon News* informed its readers that their "machine left the ground about one foot for a distance of fifty yards."[13] In Valdosta the paper carried the article under the headline "Didn't Fly Very Far,"[14] but it did fly and it was the first in the state. News of the first flight in Georgia not only appeared in papers throughout Georgia, the story was picked up by the Associated Press and distributed to newspapers across the country.[15]

There is no known edition of the *Athens Banner*, the daily newspaper in Athens, in existence for the date 30 August 1909. As a result, it remains unknown what the *Athens Banner*'s editors, Hugh Rowe and Thomas Reed, had to say about this flight, which they witnessed. However, a copy of the *Athens Weekly Banner*, printed on Friday, 3 September 1909, the first issue to appear after the historic flight, is part of the newspaper collection at the University of Georgia's main library. The *Athens Weekly Banner* carried reprints of articles of interest printed in the daily papers earlier in the week as well as original articles.

The first flight is mentioned in the 3 September 1909 weekly edition of this paper. Curiously, instead of reprinting articles about the flight that may have run early in the week, this edition only devoted two sentences to the flight and did not even name Ben or Zumpt as the two Athenians who achieved this feat. The *Athens Weekly Banner* simply stated, "Athens believes in being first in accomplishing things. While the other cities in Georgia read about the aviators, Athens had two young men at work building an aeroplane, and while it has not proved thoroughly successful, it did get off the ground a while, and gave Athens the record of having furnished the first aeroplane flight in Georgia."[16]

Sunday was the Lord's Day, a day of rest. Ben was raised a Baptist and continued in the Baptist faith his entire life. Zumpt was raised a Methodist and kept his membership in the Methodist church his entire life.[17] There would be no attempt to fly on Sunday morning. But early Monday morning, Ben and Zumpt were back in Lynwood Park with their repaired Epps-Huff III Monoplane ready for a second flight. This time the crowd ballooned to an estimated 1,000 spectators. The reporter who was present on Saturday was back to record the results of the second attempt, but the outcome this time was disappointing. Tuesday's front page of the *Atlanta Constitution* carried the dismal results:

> The second flight of the aeroplane of Ben Epps and Zump [*sic*] Huff was not as successful as the first...the aeroplane failed to leave the ground. The attempts at flight this morning were witnessed by fully a thousand people. The failure of the machine to fly is attributed to the roughness of the ground and the poor start received.
>
> Instead of having a trackway prepared, along which the machine could glide to its start, the young men chose to make the

start on the plane hillside, which had more or less unevenness.

The result was the machine got no start, and there was much lost motion. The twisting of the machine over the uneven ground caused one of the wheels to spread, and the machine was brought to a sudden stop....

[Ben and Zumpt] were not in the least daunted by their failure this morning and will try again in a few days....

They are not backed by any money, having constructed the machine out of their own wages. They have had no advantage of technical training in colleges, and the entire machine has been built by their own hands.[18]

Even though Ben and Zumpt were disappointed that they'd let down such a large crowd, the fact that the second attempt was unsuccessful was inconsequential. History had been made in Athens, Georgia, on 28 August 1909, and the flight on that day will forever remain Georgia's "first." It was an extraordinary accomplishment against incredible odds, achieved by two young men with a dream.

The magnitude of Ben and Zumpt's accomplishment was immediately realized. A few days after the first flight, the *Oglethorpe Echo* lauded Ben and Zumpt in a front-page article.

It is interesting that right here, within call of Lexington almost, a pair of aviators are [*sic*] to be found and that it is possible a successful machine to fly through space may be the outcome of their endeavors. The young flying enthusiasts are Messrs. Epps and Huff of Athens, whom some of our people know. They have not yet been successful in traveling any great distance above terra firma but the[y] are at work on the machine and hope to have a fine sail before many days. The trials are being made at Lynwood [P]ark, Athens. Attention of the whole state has been attracted and it is possible the young gentlemen may become a second pair of Wright Brothers.[19]

For Ben and Zumpt to be considered as a possible "second pair of Wright Brothers" was indeed high praise. Their names were in print across the state. Whether they wanted it or not, they were celebrities; their dream had been achieved. Although their goal had never been to set a record, they would forever be the "first" in Georgia. In fact, the flight of the Epps-Huff III on 28 August 1909 was an achievement of greater significance than even Ben or Zumpt ever realized during their lifetimes.

More Than a Georgia First

Neither Ben nor Zumpt ever heard of Henry W. Walden of Mineola, Long Island, New York. When Walden died in 1964, long after Ben's death, Zumpt was living in Florida and was not aware of Walden's obituary that ran in the *New York Times*.[20] Had Ben or Zumpt known of Walden, or had Zumpt read Walden's obituary, they would have found that he had an interest in aviation very similar to their own. Walden even started building airplanes about the same time that Ben and Zumpt started their partnership.

Henry Walden was born in Massachusetts on 10 November 1883. After earning a degree in dentistry from Columbia University in 1906, he opened a dental office in Manhattan. However, his real passion was aviation. It was a passion that began when he was a youth, fascinated with designing and building kites and balloons. His passion for aeronautics grew over the years. In 1908, Walden joined the Aeronautical Society of New York, based at the Morris Park racetrack in the Bronx. This opportunity allowed him to express his creativity, increase his knowledge of aeronautics, and experiment in designing and building his own airplanes.[21]

Walden's first two models were pusher-type biplanes, and both were failures. He switched to a monoplane for his next design. He'd grown tired of the long trips to Morris Park, so he rented a loft near his dental office where he constructed his monoplane, the Walden III. He took what he'd learned from the deficiencies in his two biplanes and incorporated these improvements into his new plane. The Walden III was a pusher-type design made of wood, cables, and fabric. The undercarriage sat on three wheels in a triangle configuration, just as Ben and Zumpt's Epps-Huff II and Epps-Huff III Monoplanes had. The Walden III was powered by a three-cylinder Anzani engine.[22]

During a trial run, Walden was successful in getting his fragile craft to rise a few feet off the ground and sustain a short, controlled flight before the plane's one-gallon gas tank ran dry. The plane traveled just over thirty feet, but it was credited with being the first manned flight of a monoplane built in the United States.[23] Eight months later, after installing a ten-gallon gas tank, Walden was able to achieve a successful flight in his Walden III that was a little longer, but this time his flight ended in a crash, with Walden breaking several ribs and fracturing his collarbone.[24]

Coming off his first successful flight, Walden was better able to handle the pain of his injuries and did recover. He went on to build nine more models of airplanes and established himself as an accomplished pilot. Walden participated in air races and air shows, surviving at least a dozen or more crashes.[25]

Henry Walden stopped flying in 1912 and concentrated on design, manufacturing, and laboratory innovations. In 1915, he invented and patented the first radio-controlled, air-to-ground missile. A model of this missile and a model of his Walden III Monoplane are on display in the Smithsonian National Air and Space Museum in Washington, DC. During World War I, Walden formed a company to manufacture aircraft wings and tails for the military and in 1929 formed Walden Aircraft, a small airplane manufacturing company, which he sold in 1932 when he returned to his dentistry practice full time.[26]

Dr. Walden's aviation achievements earned him numerous honors and membership in several exclusive, prestigious organiza-tions. He was elected to membership in the Early Birds of Aviation, Inc., at that organization's founding meeting in Chicago on 17 December 1928, that day being the twenty-fifth anniversary of the first flight of the Wright brothers at Kitty Hawk, North Carolina. The basis of membership in the Early Birds was a solo flight as a pilot prior to 17 December 1916, which was before America's entry into the First World War. Dr. Walden was also elected as a governor of this organization at its first meeting.[27] He was the guest of honor at a meeting of the Early Birds held to commemorate the fiftieth anniversary of his first flight in a monoplane and received a bronze plaque for his contributions to aviation.[28] But Walden's greatest recognition was yet to occur.

On 13 September 1964, Henry W. Walden died, one week before he was inducted into the National Aviation Hall of Fame at the United States Air Force Museum in Dayton, Ohio (the "NAHF"). At the NAHF, Walden is listed as an inventor and is recognized for having built and flown the first successful monoplane in the United States—a feat he achieved on *9 December 1909*. But Walden's national record-setting flight did not occur until 106 days *after* Georgia's version of the Wright brothers, Ben Epps and Zumpt Huff, achieved the successful flight of their Epps-Huff III Monoplane.

The flight of 150 feet achieved by the Epps-Huff III Monoplane in Lynwood Park on 28 August 1909 was hailed across the state as the first flight of an airplane in the state of Georgia. Based on the date of Henry W. Walden's first flight, it was Ben and Zumpt who made the first flight of a monoplane in the United States, not Walden! Amazingly, it only took nine months for Ben and Zumpt to design, build, and fly the nation's first successful monoplane. But there's even more to the story of Ben and Zumpt's first flight.

The flight in Lynwood Park in August 1909, which was lauded in newspapers around the state, was the first successful flight of a monoplane in the United States conducted in *public*. But this publicly announced flight was not the first time that the Epps-Huff III had flown successfully. The first time this monoplane achieved a successful flight was in an earlier, *private* trial.

The Private Trial

Lola Trammell alluded to an earlier private trial of the Epps-Huff III in an article she wrote for the *Atlanta Journal Magazine* in March 1949. Like every article about Georgia's first flight since the *Atlanta Constitution* article in 1930, Trammell stated that the first flight occurred in 1907. Also, as with other journalists, she did not mention Zumpt Huff's role, nor did she state where the flight took place. But her article is one of the few that mentions an earlier private trial of the Epps-Huff III. She writes that it was "not learn[ed] until years later that young Epps had waked up a couple of pals at 2 o'clock in the moonlit morning and had slipped out to the field for a preliminary test. The plane flew fine—then."[1]

Thomas Reed said that he witnessed this private trial and described the trial in an article published three weeks before Trammell's article. Reed recalled that Ben had come to the *Athens Banner* offices, around the corner on North Lumpkin Street, and invited Reed and his boss, Hugh Rowe, to come out "that night and witness the initial flight of his machine, the construction of which he had just finished."[2] Reed described what happened:

> It was a clear night with a full moon, an ideal setting for the experiment. We went out to an open field about a block or two beyond Milledge Avenue...the land selected was open with a fairly good incline to an open field down hill to the west.
>
> Rowe and myself simply stood by and watched to see what Ben was going to do with his machine. The first attempt to get the machine off the ground and into the air failed. The second attempt was successful.

The machine got up about forty to fifty feet in the air and maintained its flight about one hundred yards. Then it came down and as it hit the ground lost both of its wings, but Epps very luckily was not even scratched.[3]

It is clear from this article that Reed considered the private trial of the Epps-Huff III as the "first" flight. Hugh Rowe's 1939 article about the "first" flight makes no mention of the trial occurring at night and says that a "large group" was present to watch. The reason for the numerous and seemingly irreconcilable differences between these two eyewitness accounts of the "first flight" is because Reed and Rowe are not describing the same event. Rowe is describing the first public trial that took place later that Saturday, after sunrise, and Reed is describing a private trial that took place the same day, in the predawn hours.

Reed also told Omie Epps, Ben's wife, his account of witnessing the nighttime, private trial in a conversation he had with Omie two months after the publication of Rowe's 1939 article. As the widow of Ben Epps, Omie was interviewed in March 1939 as part of the WPA Federal Writers' Project Interviews for a "Life Histories" article. This was a federal project instituted by the Roosevelt administration during the Great Depression. The Work Progress Administration (later known as the Work Projects Administration, the "WPA") helped to put people back to work, in part by hiring writers to collect and preserve folklore.[4]

In her interview for this project, Omie states that she had only recently heard for the first time about this earlier private trial, telling her interviewer, "Several days ago Dr. Reid [sic] told me that he and Mr. Hugh Rowe went out with Ben at two o'clock one morning to fly his first plane."[5] Omie also confirmed at the time she was interviewed that the first flight took place in "1909."[6]

Reed's conversation with Omie and subsequent article confirm what Ben and Zumpt told a reporter after the second trial on 30 August 1909. A reporter for the *Atlanta Georgian & News* had perhaps the scoop of the two-day trails, being the only paper to carry Ben and Zumpt's account of the earlier, private trial.

> Lynwood [P]ark, on the outskirts of Athens, was the scene of the first flight at 3 o'clock Saturday morning. Clearly visible in the moonlight, a strange-looking bird-like affair skimmed the ground swiftly, while the sputtering sound of a powerful engine could be heard for some distance. It was the first trial of the monoplane which has been constructed in Athens by Ben T. Eppes [sic] and Zump [sic] Huff....
> [T]he machine more than fulfilled the expectations of the young aviators, tho an unforeseen accident cut short the trial before the aeroplane had done more than barely skim the earth for about 100 yards on its first trip. The front wheel of the machine ran into a terrace, which was not clearly visible in the moonlight, and was put out of commission so that the aviators were unable to make another start.[7]

Prior to the late-night trial, Ben and Zumpt were confident that their Epps-Huff III Monoplane, which incorporated all that they'd learned from the previous two models, would fly when they announced that the first public trial would be held on the morning of 28 August 1909. This latest model was lighter, sturdier, and built to react better to the controls. The wingspan was narrowed and its chord length shortened. But it had yet to be tested in the field.

As the day for the trial drew near, they had second thoughts about a public trial before testing the Epps-Huff III in private. On 27 August, at the eleventh hour, Ben and Zumpt hastily arranged a private test in the darkness of the early morning hours before the public test. They checked the evening weather forecast. The sky would be clear, no wind, and most important, a full moon. The conditions were ideal.

Ben went to the *Athens Banner* office, around the corner from Epps Garage, to invite Hugh Rowe and Thomas Reed to the private trial that night. Ben and Zumpt wanted two prominent, pillars of the community as witnesses to this flight to give independent confirmation of the plane's success. Rowe was a few months away from being elected to his first of two terms as mayor of Athens, and Reed would assume the position of registrar at the University of Georgia in November, a position he would hold until 1945. Rowe and Reed would be excellent witnesses and could vouch for the success of the Epps-Huff III in the event that it crashed at the end of the private trial and was not able to fly at the public trial.

Both Ben and Zumpt went home for dinner after making plans to meet at the garage later that evening. When they met back at the garage, they spent the remaining hours before the planned private trial making final arrangements. They checked and rechecked every inch of their plane. There was no time for sleep and the adrenaline rush from the anticipation wouldn't have allowed them to sleep anyway.

The private trial was set for three o'clock in the morning. No one would be out on the streets to see them hauling the plane from the garage to Lynwood Park, nor would anyone be in the park at that hour. But Ben and Zumpt were concerned about the noise the plane would make in the park. It was a hot, humid August night and windows would be open. The dray carrying the monoplane to Lynwood Park would creak and strain as it rolled past Ben's parents's home and the other homes spread along West Hancock Avenue. And when the engine was cranked and revved, the noise would carry for more than a mile through the still night air. It would be a noise unlike any ever heard in this neighborhood. With his parents sleeping only blocks away, Ben could only hope that it was a deep sleep at 3:00 A.M.

There is no indication as to whether the noise from the private trial awakened Ben's parents that morning, but there were a number of homes much closer to the takeoff location, and the deafening roar of the engine surely caused bewilderment and fear in those households. They were suddenly awakened, at an ungodly hour, by a loud noise that had never before been heard in their neighborhood.

Besides being the only newspaper to cover the account of the earlier, private trial, the *Atlanta Georgian & News* was the only publication ever, before now, a span of more than one hundred years, to report that Ben was not the only one onboard the Epps-Huff III when it made its first flight. After cranking the propeller, Zumpt ducked under the wing and squeezed in next to Ben on the wagon seat. "[B]oth were aboard and the machine more than fulfilled the expectations of the young aviators," when the Epps-Huff III left the ground and made its first flight, traveling a distance of 300 feet.[8]

The damage to the plane was not significant when the front wheel struck a terrace they were not able to see, even with the moonlight, and ended the flight. It didn't take long to load the Epps-Huff III onto the dray and haul it back to the garage for repairs so it would be ready for the public trial shortly after dawn. Ben and Zumpt were normally quiet individuals, taciturn to an extreme. They rarely started a conversation or had much to say when engaged, but on that ride back to the garage, they weren't able to contain their smiles, laughter, and sheer exuberance. Triumphant shouts of joy pierced the predawn darkness.

The repairs were quickly made. Neither Ben nor Zumpt would make any attempt to sleep. The adrenaline rush was even more pronounced than before, which didn't seem possible. They'd just flown their first flight, which they knew was the first flight in the state, in a plane that they'd built on their own. Their dream had been realized. It was one of the most remarkable feats in Georgia history. It was a time to celebrate, not to sleep. The Epps-Huff partnership forged ahead.

More Trials, Another Epps-Huff Design

At the conclusion of the second public trial on Monday, 30 August 1909, the damaged Epps-Huff III was again hauled back to the garage. It took little time to repair the bicycle wheel that spread from the frame. Ben and Zumpt checked the plane thoroughly for other damage and tightened the cable wires. It was as good as new and ready for the next trial, but they didn't rush back to Lynwood Park. Instead, they looked for a solution to the problem that the uneven ground caused in slowing the Epps-Huff III and hampering its ability to gain speed and lift.

The Wright brothers had not encountered this problem. Their 1903 Wright Flyer did not have wheels, it was launched from a rail that provided a smooth run while the plane built sufficient speed to lift.

The Athens paper announced the solution that Ben and Zumpt settled on.

> The two young inventors of Athens who have created so much excitement with the trials of their monoplane are having a wooden track laid on the hill which was the scene of their former efforts to fly, and when the new propellers are in shape and the machine ready for another attempt the track will be completed.[1]

The uneven ground was not the only concern that needed to be addressed before another trial was attempted. Ben and Zumpt were also worried about the crowds that their Saturday and Monday trials had attracted. None of the spectators had witnessed a plane taking off before and were not sure what to expect or how to react. Several spectators, including small children, ran across the field in front of the Epps-Huff III as it began its run down the slope from Hill Street. Most were oblivious to the dangers they risked as they crossed perilously close to the plane and its spinning propeller. There was also the ever-present fear of an explosion and fire. They couldn't risk a serious injury to one or perhaps many of these spectators if the plane crashed and exploded. The decision was made to conduct the trials in private, at least for the foreseeable future.

The paper was also acutely aware of the spectator problem.

> Eppes [*sic*] and Huff have not announced whether their attempt will be a public one or not, but at the last trial the crowd interfered considerably with the trial of the monoplane, and it is likely that the next attempt which will be held this week will be in private.[2]

It's not known how many additional trials the Epps-Huff III may have made that fall. These trials were conducted in private and there was no reporting of the outcome in the newspapers. The wooden track that was built on the hillside in Lynwood Park apparently did little to improve the performance of the plane, since it was still experiencing problems getting off the ground. When the Epps-Huff III crashed in Lynwood Park yet again that fall, the decision was made not to rebuild it. As with the previous models that had not achieved the success they were striving for, Ben and Zumpt refused to let their enthusiasm and optimism be diminished. Their response was the same as before: they went to work on a new, improved model, one that incorporated all they had learned from the Epps-Huff III.

By mid-fall 1909, the Epps-Huff III, the first monoplane to fly in the United States, was unceremoniously dismantled in the garage on East Washington Street and the parts that could be reused would soon be incorporated into the next monoplane of the Epps-Huff partnership. The monoplane that made state and national history would not end up in the Smithsonian National Air and Space Museum in Washington, DC, alongside other historic aircraft to be displayed to future generations; nor would it be housed in the Museum of Aviation Aircraft and Missiles, in Warner Robbins, home to the Georgia Aviation Hall of Fame. Instead, the Epps-Huff III became a pile of disassembled parts spread across the floor of Epps Garage, waiting to be worked into the next model design of the Epps-Huff partnership.

This was a big loss for historical preservation and for future generations who would've loved seeing this monoplane. But Ben and Zumpt didn't have the luxury, the space, or the money to hold on to it. And making or preserving history was never what their venture was about. They weren't looking for rewards, accolades, or acclaim. Ben and Zumpt were focused on results and looking to achieve greater success.

As cold weather settled on Athens, Ben and Zumpt withdrew into Epps Garage, continuing to work nights and weekends and exchanging ideas on how to improve their design to achieve the level of flight they were seeking. They concluded that the last model was still too heavy and unwieldy to get very far off the ground or travel long distances. Due to a shortage of funds, they had used cheap materials in the construction of their previous models. They'd learned a lot from their mistakes and decided that if they were going to achieve the success they were aiming for, they had to use better quality materials. They worked long hours to make the next model lighter and better balanced. It would also be constructed with higher quality and stronger materials.

The new model, the Epps-Huff IV, had a similar look to the Epps-Huff III. It was a monoplane with an undercarriage of three bicycle wheels, a rear, single-plane rudder and double-plane elevator in front. But this model was smaller than the last. The span of the wing was reduced again, this time to twenty-four feet. The main body was shortened to six feet, with the pilot's seat moved back so that it was positioned between the back two bicycle wheels. The propeller was shortened to four feet. Construction of the Epps-Huff IV Monoplane was completed before the end of 1909 and ready to be rolled out and tested on the street.

When their workday ended on 31 December 1909, Ben and Zumpt met at the garage. They had no plans for a revelrous New Year's Eve celebration; they had something else in mind. They were now being referred to as the "young inventors" and were anxiously waiting for East Washington Street to empty of traffic so they could roll out their latest invention. They were hoping not to attract a crowd.

At 5:30 P.M. they moved the Epps-Huff IV Monoplane onto the street for its first test run. The engine was not yet installed, but they wanted to test this new model as a glider to see how well it handled with the adjustments they'd made. The plane was pulled up and down Washington Street in front of Epps Garage from College Avenue down to Pulaski Street and then back to College Avenue.

The sight of the new monoplane on the street quickly drew the crowd they'd hoped to avoid. It seemed that not everyone had gone home to get ready for New Year's Eve celebrations. The plane was described as a type used by Glenn Curtiss and Frenchman Louis Paulhan, although their models were biplanes. It reminded one reporter, who came out to see what was drawing the crowd, of "a white-winged birdlike craft gliding down Washington St."[3]

Comparing this model to the earlier Epps-Huff III, the Epps-Huff IV was described by this reporter as having "a smaller plane surface than the first machine. It is, however, far better balanced and of much superior construction and better and lighter materials...so that the second machine is an improvement over the first one [to fly]."[4] Coming off its first public appearance and test, the headline on page one of the Athens paper on the first day of the new year, 1910, read, "Aeroplane Tested on City Streets, Messrs. Huff and Eppes [sic] Have Finished Second Monoplane and Will Try It Soon."[5]

One week after the initial public street trial, an Athens reporter followed up on the work being done on the Epps-Huff IV Monoplane. His article provided more details about the construction of the new plane than any previous article about an Epps-Huff design. He described what he saw when he inspected the Epps-Huff IV:

> The monoplane now being constructed is a curious looking craft, with the clean-cut lines of a racing yacht...the main plane is six by twenty-four feet and is stoutly braced, while the two front planes, arranged on the order of the Wright biplane, provide the tilting of the monoplane upward or downward...the two front planes, which have the appearance of a box kite, though longer, are three by eight feet, and the steering of the aircraft is done by a wide flat single plane rudder, located ten feet back of the main plane and the driver's seat.
>
> This is controlled from the seat, as are the front double plane...the start is provided for by having the monoplane supported from the ground by three strong bicycle wheels placed in the form of a triangle, one under the front and two under the driver's seat and balancing the main plane.[6]

At the time that this article was written, Ben and Zumpt had installed an 8-horsepower engine in the plane. This was sufficient to drive the two-bladed, four-foot propeller with "terrific speed," but was acknowledged to be insufficient to enable the plane to fly. Plans were made to install a more powerful engine before the plane was taken to Lynwood Park for trials.

Once again, Ben and Zumpt would build a wooden track down the hillside in the park to launch their latest model. Trials of the plane were to begin before the end of January, and like the recent trials of their last model, the Epps-Huff III, these trials would be held in secret. But this time, Ben and Zumpt promised the citizens of Athens that "if the machine comes up to expectation it will be given a public trial soon afterwards."[7]

Disappointingly, the Epps-Huff IV did not live up to expectation. After installing a 20-horsepower engine in the Epps-Huff IV, it was tested several times without making a single successful flight. On 24 February 1910, Ben and Zumpt loaded their Epps-Huff IV in front of the garage on East Washington Street for yet one more field trial.

> The monoplane was loaded on a dray, just as if it had been a boat, and transported to the trial grounds. The sight of the trim and neat looking flying machine, perched on top of the dray, with the sleepy horse standing waiting for his driver to start him, attracted no little attention on Washington street yesterday afternoon and there was quite a crowd collected to watch the departure for the trial grounds. It was somewhat of a reversal of the usual catch word, which is so often applied to the modern automobile in time of trouble, but the crowd caught the spirit of the things and cried, "Get a horse." The test was made yesterday afternoon, and according to reports received last night was not a success, for the monoplane failed to get off the ground and although the more powerful motor propelled it along the ground swiftly it did not possess enough strength to fly.[8]

This latest attempt to fly the Epps-Huff IV was no more successful than the other attempts. There was no reason to believe that one more attempt would result in a different outcome. For just over one year, Ben and Zumpt had been building planes that were pusher-type planes, as Glenn Curtiss and his A.E.A. group were building in New York. Except for the limited success they had with the Epps-Huff III Monoplane in Lynwood Park in August 1909, Ben and Zumpt were not at all satisfied with the progress they were making. It was time for the Epps-Huff partnership to switch to a new design, one that would be a radical departure for the partnership.

The decision was made before spring arrived to abandon the pusher-type design they'd been using from the beginning and build, instead, a plane that was a tractor-type design. An airplane constructed with a tractor configuration has the engine mounted with the propeller facing forward, so that the aircraft is "pulled" through the air. This is the opposite of the pusher configuration, in which the propeller is in the aft position and "pushes" the airplane through the air. The partnership would never return to a pusher configuration again.

Ben and Zumpt knew exactly what their next model would look like. While building their first monoplane, the Epps-Huff II, they had no photograph of a monoplane to use to model their design. The design of the Epps-Huff II had come solely from Ben's creativity. But after designing and building the Epps-Huff II, they heard about a tractor-type monoplane that had been built by a Frenchman. They wrote to this Frenchman, who had already achieved worldwide fame as an aviator, and asked if he would send a photograph of his latest tractor-type design monoplane.

By the time this letter from Athens, Georgia, was received in France, this aviator was in the process of readying for an attempt at a feat that no aviator in the world had accomplished. Helping the Frenchman in this endeavor was an Italian with a name Ben and Zumpt knew well.

Despite being heavily involved in preparing for an aviation world record, the Frenchman took the time to send Ben and Zumpt the photograph they requested. With this photograph in hand, Ben and Zumpt were ready to start building a similarly styled, tractor-type monoplane in Athens. The new design would look totally different from any plane the Epps-Huff partnership had ever built. Both Ben and Zumpt felt this new design was the look of the future of aviation, and they were eager to join aviators around the world who were working to build successful monoplanes similar to the Frenchman's.

The Switch to a Tractor-Type Design

Spring was approaching when the Epps-Huff IV was hauled back to the garage for the last time, after its latest crash. Ben and Zumpt made the decision that it would not be rebuilt. With the start of a new season, it was time for a new design. They'd been discussing a change in design for months and knew exactly what they wanted to build. They'd read about a plane that had been built in France that was attracting a lot of attention. It was a monoplane known as the Blériot XI, built by the Frenchman Louis Blériot.

Blériot was an inventor and engineer born in Cambrai, France, in 1872. He gained fame and a fortune from inventing automobile headlights and established an acetylene headlamp business. He used his fortune to experiment with towing gliders on the Seine River to learn about airplanes and aerodynamics. Between 1903 and 1906 he collaborated with another inventor to build several unsuccessful airplane designs. He left that venture to form his own company and continued to experiment with various configurations.

Louis Blériot created and flew the world's first successful monoplane, the Blériot V, on 5 April 1907. It was a flight of only twenty feet, but it was the first time that one of Blériot's models had ever flown successfully. The Blériot V was a pusher-type model, powered by a 24-horsepower, Antoinette water-cooled engine. The engine was mounted behind the wing and the propeller faced aft. The Blériot V crashed 19 April 1907 and was destroyed.[1]

Blériot continued building new models, improving them with what he learned from previous models. In 1908, he built the Blériot XI, a light, sleek monoplane constructed of oak and poplar wood. The wing and front half of the fuselage were covered with cloth. By leaving the aft section of the fuselage uncovered, Blériot unintentionally created enough drag to add to the lateral stability of the plane. The plane used wing warping to control roll. The tail section included a horizontal stabilizer with an elevator and a rudder but no vertical stabilizer. This monoplane was a tractor-type design, whereby the engine was mounted on the front of the plane with the propeller facing forward and operating to pull the plane forward.[2]

The Blériot XI made its first public appearance at an air show in Paris in December 1908. It was powered by an R.E.P. engine and had a four-blade metal, paddle-type propeller. It flew for the first time on 23 January 1909. But both the engine and propeller proved unsatisfactory to Blériot. In spring 1909, he consulted with Alessandro Anzani and refitted the Blériot XI with a 25-horsepower Anzani three-cylinder engine and a two-blade Chauviere wooden propeller. The plane demonstrated significant improvement. Blériot was so pleased with the performance of the Blériot XI that he announced he would compete for the £1,000 prize offered by the London *Daily Mail* for the first airplane to successfully fly across the English Channel.[3]

Ben and Zumpt were impressed with what they'd read about the Blériot XI. In June 1909, while they experimented with their Epps-Huff II, they wrote to Louis Blériot. In response, Blériot sent a photograph of his Blériot XI. Zumpt's scrapbook has a copy of the photograph of the Blériot XI that they received. Zumpt typed on this photograph,

> June 1909, Ben Epps and I read of a Frenchman Louis Bleriot had [*sic*] built a palne [*sic*], a monoplane, in which he was or wanted to fly across the English Chanel [*sic*] in it. We immediately wrote to him for a photograph of his Monoplane we [*sic*] received this photo from him July sometime. This plane was as shown, it was powered by an Air Cooled Anzani 25 h.p. engine four cylinder, his speed was about 45 miles per hour. We Owned [*sic*] an Anzani Twin Cylinder Motor Cycle [*sic*] Engine with

which after some alterations made by Ben Epps he was able to lift his plane from the [*sic*] for his First Flight a little later on after Bleriot flew the English Channel. Zumpt Alston Huff.[4]

On 25 July 1909, with Alessandro Anzani present to ensure that his engine was operating at peak performance, Louis Blériot took off from Calais, France, in his Blériot XI. Despite the fog and bad weather, in just over thirty-six minutes Blériot landed in Dover, England. It was the first crossing of a large body of water in a heavier-than-air machine and earned Blériot the £1,000 prize money. For his part, the performance earned Anzani a flood of orders for both airplane and motorcycle engines.[5]

Construction of the next Epps-Huff-designed monoplane, based on the Blériot XI, was finished by late spring 1910. The new plane, the Epps-Huff V, had a single set of parasol wings attached high on a square-shaped, open-frame fuselage. Only the underside of the wings was "skinned" with fabric. Wing warping was again used to control roll. The new design was operated by a steering wheel instead of a tee-bar, which had been used on previous models. The biggest design change was the placement of the engine. For the first time, the engine was placed in front of the wing with the propeller set in the forward position. In this manner, the plane is "pulled" forward; it was a tractor configuration. One of the things that Ben and Zumpt quickly learned from this design was that the monoplane "could be pulled faster than driven, the 'Pusher' type." They forever abandoned the pusher design.[6]

The Epps-Huff V had four wheels, all the same size. Two wheels were positioned under the engine, attached to a narrow, rectangular frame. The other two wheels were positioned under the tail section. Two wood landing skids were added on the outside of the front wheels. The Epps-Huff V had a more modern, "standard" arrangement where both the elevator and rudder were in the tail section. The gas tank was positioned above the wing, over the engine, and in front of the steering wheel. There were three king posts coming to a point above the gas tank, creating a tripod design. Wire cabling was strung from the king posts to various points along the two spars near the leading edge and trailing edge of the wings. The underside of the wings was cabled to the open fuselage. The Epps-Huff V would make its first public appearance at the new Davis-Escoe horse track in Athens.

Construction on the Davis-Escoe racetrack began in early 1910. It was a half-mile, circular track with stables located on Barber Street. The facility was to be used to train local horses and to attract a number of East Coast horses for the winter training season, making Athens a center for horsemen during the winter season. The facility offered trotting, running, and harness events and, it was hoped, would make Athens a center for the sporting gentry.[7]

The new track opened on 28 June 1910 with two pacing races scheduled, each being the best three-out-of-five, one-mile heats. The third event was a two-heat, half-mile trotting race. In between the races there were exhibition runs of automobiles, which were furnished by Bishop Motor Cars and Epps Garage. Along with this bill of fare, it was announced that a "demonstration of an aeroplane" was being added "for good measure."[8]

The event was attended by 1,500 spectators, with scores of those being ladies who were carried to the new track in "autos and buggies, carriages and tallyhos." The "grand stand and judges stand were gaily decorated for the occasion," and bright flags were placed at intervals around the track. The crowd was reported to be "one of the largest ever seen at an Athens track" and the regalement was even better than advertised. The crowd showed great interest in the demonstration of the Epps-Huff V. The four-wheel monoplane rolled onto the track in front of the grandstand. The demonstration was described the next day:

> The machine seems practical in every respect except the motor is a little too heavy or a little too weak. The machine on its landing roller-wheels glided over the ground at a fair rate of speed

and was easily guided by the operator. It did not, however, rise in the air. Many express their confidence in the scientific practicability in the main idea of the machine and with some improvement on the motive power it will doubtless be able to make trips through the cerulean all right.[9]

Although the Epps-Huff V did not fly at the Davis-Escoe track demonstration, Zumpt recorded that this plane was also taken to Lynwood Park for trials. There are photographs of the Epps-Huff V in Lynwood Park in Zumpt's scrapbook and Ben's scrapbook. The date "1910" is handwritten above the wing on the photograph of the plane in Ben's scrapbook.[10] On the copy of this photograph that is in Zumpt's scrapbook, the date was altered by Zumpt to read "1909." Based on the previously cited newspaper article from 1910, the date on the photograph in Ben's scrapbook is correct.[11] On the same page of Ben's scrapbook there is a photograph of the Epps-Huff V Monoplane after a crash in Lynwood Park, possibly its last crash. In this photograph, the tail section is torn off and sits perpendicular to the fuselage.[12]

There is also a photograph of the Epps-Huff V Monoplane on a dirt road with a horse-drawn dray following behind, in Zumpt's collage (Image Number 18). Zumpt typed, "Here Ben Epps...placed the engine and the propeller in front" on the photo. The road is described by Zumpt as being "on the east side of Lynwood Park."[13] If he is correct in his placement of this road, the Epps-Huff V Monoplane was on Billups Street and would have been a block and a half from Ben's parents's house. The elevated dirt bank in the photograph on the right side of the plane is still present today running along the east side of Billups Street.

The design of the Epps-Huff V, and in particular the switch to a tractor-type configuration, proved far superior to the old pusher-type models. However, the performance of the Epps-Huff V still did not reach the level that Ben and Zumpt were looking to achieve. When this model crashed in late summer or early fall 1910, the decision was made to use the parts to build another tractor-type monoplane, with a few structural changes.

Ben and Zumpt worked together during fall 1910 on a model that would be the Epps-Huff VI Monoplane. In this design, the front wheelbase was widened for better balance when landing. The two landing skids that had been placed on the outside of the front wheels were replaced with a single skid centered between the front wheels. As with the Epps-Huff V, the tail section was supported by two wheels. Instead of the tripod-configured king posts, the Epps-Huff VI had four king posts coming to a point above the gas tank, over the engine. The six-foot propeller was replaced with a four-foot propeller. The fuselage was again square shaped, with the pilot's seat sitting low so that the steering wheel was above the pilot's head. There is a photograph in Ben's scrapbook of the Epps-Huff VI flying several feet above the ground over an open field.[14]

Although photographs indicate that this plane flew well, it apparently met with the same fate as its predecessors. After a crash in late fall, the parts were used to begin construction of a new model, the seventh design, which was finished in February 1911. But before the model VII was finished, some major changes occurred within the Epps-Huff partnership.

As 1910 was drawing to a close, it became apparent to Ben that his garage, automobile, motorcycle, bicycle, and airplane businesses had outgrown the small confines of the premises at 120 East Washington Street. He began looking for a larger facility to accommodate all of these varied business interests. In late November 1910, he found what he was looking for down the street, beyond College Avenue, at 392 East Washington Street. The location was across from the Georgian Hotel and a block farther down. By 1 December 1910, Ben had moved into the new location and was advertising Michelin tires for sale at "Epps Garage, 392 Washington Street."[15] The other, and more significant, change for the partnership was that Zumpt had moved to Atlanta by 1911.[16]

Building airplanes was expensive and time consuming. Neither Ben nor Zumpt had the financial means to turn their airplane hobby into a commercial enterprise, nor did either come from a family in a financial position to help. No wealthy investors were found or stepped forward to finance a commercial venture. Both knew that without a significant infusion of money, their hobby would remain little more than a hobby. If either of them were contemplating having a family, he knew their airplane partnership wouldn't support a wife and children.[17] They'd spent countless hours for two full years designing, building, and testing different models, and although their dream of achieving a sustained, controlled flight in a heavier-than-air machine had been realized, their venture had not generated one penny of income. The money always flowed out, never in to the partnership. It wasn't financially feasible for the partnership to go forward.

A contributing factor to the partnership's financial problems was the economy, which proved to be a headwind as strong as those sometimes faced by their planes. Shortly after the partnership achieved its first flight, the country entered a recession. Called the Panic of 1910, it was a mild recession compared to others, but it was a lengthy one. It lasted from January 1910 to January 1912. The Epps-Huff partnership found itself developing its flying machines in pursuit of a commercial venture in the heart of the Panic of 1910.[18]

Before the start of 1911, the Epps-Huff partnership ended. In its first nine short months of existence, this partnership had attained the seemingly impossible for two young men from Athens. But just as quickly as it rose in fame, the memory of this partnership's existence and accomplishments faded. This remarkable story was forgotten.

With the publication of the August 1909 newspaper articles around the state about the first flight of the Epps-Huff III Monoplane and the two partners being referenced as "a second pair of Wright Brothers," Ben and Zumpt gained instant fame. Any time they appeared in public they were acknowledged as celebrity inventors. Even seemingly inconsequential outings by Ben or Zumpt became noteworthy of reporting.

In the latter part of 1909, Zumpt's family moved to Oglethorpe County, while Zumpt and his sister, Floy, remained in Athens living in a boarding house.[19] On an occasion when Zumpt traveled to Oglethorpe County to visit his parents, the *Oglethorpe Echo* deemed this a noteworthy event and advised it readers, "Mr. Zumpt Huff, the airship inventor from Athens, came down to visit his parents Mr. and Mrs. A. J. [*sic*] Huff, Sunday."[20]

One day Ben was driving back from Atlanta in a new Ford automobile. He was between Bogart and Athens when a rabbit came out of the brush and took off down the road. Sadly, the rabbit wasn't fast enough to outrun Ben's car and the rabbit's running days ended. The unfortunate, seemingly innocuous incident was splashed across page two of the *Athens Weekly Banner* under the headline "Ben Epps Flying Machine Inventor Ran Over a Rabbit on Road in Auto."[21] Six months later, Ben was in the paper again, this time for breaking his arm while cranking another man's car engine.[22]

But with the demise of the partnership, its existence and the story of the first flight faded quickly. Several factors contributed to this happening, including the fact that neither Ben nor Zumpt took any steps to keep their accomplishment before the public. They didn't travel around the state giving talks about their accomplishment, nor did they do this around Athens. They never wrote about their accomplishment or granted interviews. There was no thought given to designing a well-planned public relations campaign or hiring a promotional agent. They showed no interest in publicity of any kind. Although they were friendly by nature, both were quiet and would never engage in, much less initiate, conversations about themselves or their achievements. Years later, Ben's wife would describe his tendency to never talk to her about his achievements; instead, what he did was cut out newspaper articles about himself and his planes and bring home for her to read.[23]

The Epps-Huff partnership never came up with a design, a system, or a component part that was unique or a "first" that advanced the development of the airplane, which would have kept the partnership's legacy alive. As the months passed after their initial flight, these two pioneers found themselves working in an aviation field that was becoming more accepted and "commonplace." They were no longer achieving feats "never-before-seen" or worthy of generating statewide publicity.

Ben and Zumpt did achieve the phenomenal feat of building and flying not only the first airplane in Georgia, but also the first flight of a monoplane in the United States. It was an accomplishment that not even the Wright brothers had achieved. However, neither Ben nor Zumpt nor anyone else at the time was aware of this national record, which would have drawn national attention for their partnership. One article at the time did proffer that their flight was the first monoplane flight in the South, but no one ever took the time to check further.[24]

After the newspaper articles of late August 1909, the date of 28 August 1909 was never published again as the date of the first flight in Georgia. There is no evidence that there was any mention of the historic flight on any of its subsequent anniversaries prior to the twentieth, at which time the *Athens Banner-Herald* referenced this milestone on its front page on 4 August 1929 under the headline, "The Birth of Aviation in Athens...Twenty Years Ago." Below the headline was the quintessential photograph of Ben in front of his shop standing next to the Epps-Huff II Monoplane. The caption under the photograph reads, "It is one of the first in this section of the country and was built by Ben Epps in his garage back in 1909. The plane never was a success but the builder was willing to risk his neck in it—and did."[25] This was the full extent of the twentieth anniversary notation. There was no mention that the first flight took place on 28 August 1909 in Lynwood Park and no mention of Zumpt Huff or his contribution to the first flight.

In 1923, Hugh Rowe, having served two terms as mayor of Athens and working at that time as editor of the *Athens Banner-Herald*, wrote a history of Athens and Clarke County. Although he was an eyewitness to history being made when Ben and Zumpt flew the first flight, there is no mention in his book that the first airplane to fly in Georgia did so in Athens, Clarke County, nor is there any mention of Ben or Zumpt in his book.[26]

There wasn't even a mention of the first flight when Ben died in October 1937 in an airplane crash. One of the articles about his death only points out that Ben "was a pioneer in the field of aviation."[27] A caption under a photograph of Ben's crashed plane came closest to acknowledging Ben's achievements by describing him as "among Georgia's first aviators, if not the first."[28] Similarly, Ben's obituary made no mention of the first flight or the date he achieved this feat.[29]

It wasn't until long after Ben's death that journalists began to appreciate the magnitude of what had been accomplished with the success of that first flight. By the time this appreciation began to grow, the two articles in August 1909 that appeared in the *Atlanta Constitution* had long been buried in the newspaper's archives and forgotten, as had the articles that appeared that month and year in Augusta, Macon, Savannah, and Valdosta newspapers.

The *Oglethorpe Echo* carried a reprint of its article of 3 September 1909 on 6 September 1984. The reprint appeared under the title "Echoes from the Past, 75 Years Ago, September 3, 1909,"[30] along with other articles from the 3 September 1909 paper. This was the article that named the "young flying machine enthusiasts...Messrs. Epps and Huff of Athens" and complimented them by stating, "The young gentlemen may become a second pair of Wright Brothers." But there was no comment or explanation accompanying the 1984 reprinted article and no one grasped its significance.[31]

Also forgotten was the role Zumpt played in the first flight. After Zumpt moved to Atlanta before the end of 1910, there was never a published mention of the Epps-Huff partnership, except for the *Oglethorpe Echo*'s 1984 reprint from its 3 September 1909 paper.

At the time of Ben's death, Zumpt, his wife, and two daughters were living in Florida, where Zumpt would live for the rest of his life, for almost four more decades. There was still time for Zumpt to revive the memory of the Epps-Huff partnership and record the correct account of who, when, and where the first airplane flight in the state of Georgia occurred. Zumpt was the one person who knew the complete story and could preserve this important event for the annals of the state's and nation's history.

Zumpt A. Huff: The Post-Partnership Years

The Epps-Huff partnership ended when Zumpt Huff moved to Atlanta. In 1911, he was living on Marietta Street. Using the experience he gained from working at the Crystal Theatre in Athens, he found a job as the operator of the A La Mode Theatre, a motion picture theater on Whitehall Street.[1] Like his father had done while Zumpt was growing up, Zumpt moved frequently during his years in Atlanta. He never owned his residence; instead, he lived in boarding houses, apartments, or rental houses. He also changed jobs frequently.

In 1912, Zumpt was living on W. Merritts Avenue and working at the Majestic Theater on Peachtree Street.[2] By 1913, Zumpt had moved to Jonesboro Drive.[3] A year later he was living on Houston Street and working at the Montgomery Theater on Auburn Avenue.[4] By the start of 1915, he'd moved once again, this time to a boarding house on Walton Street. He'd also switched jobs again and was now working at the Alamo Theater No. 2.[5]

While Zumpt was moving around Atlanta, his father and the rest of his family were also on the move, promoting his father's "Balm of Gilead" tonic medicine. When his family moved to Oglethorpe County in the latter part of 1909, his father turned most of the responsibility for his photography business over to two of Zumpt's sisters, Myrtle ("Myrt") and Nell, while his father concentrated on selling his tonic.[6]

The year 1915 brought significant changes in Zumpt's life. On 15 August of that year, he married Ellen Roberta Eubanks in Decatur, Georgia.[7] Zumpt and Roberta lived on Oakhurst Street in Atlanta, and before the end of that year, Zumpt started an electrical contracting business. It was a partnership operating under the name Huff-Schneider Electrical Company of Atlanta.[8]

Major changes in Zumpt's life continued. He and Roberta became parents on 19 June 1916 with the birth of a daughter, Katherine Maureen Huff.[9] The following spring Zumpt's father, who'd moved back to Athens, became seriously ill. Zumpt traveled to Athens to help care for him. He realized that his father was too ill to stay at home. After some convincing, Zumpt talked his father into coming to Atlanta and being admitted to Georgia Baptist Hospital.

James Huff's condition took a turn for the worse, and after only a few days at Georgia Baptist he died on 9 April 1917, at the age of fifty-nine.[10] After his father's death, Zumpt moved his stepmother, a sister, brother, and half-sister into his and Roberta's home in Atlanta until he could find a place nearby for them to live.[11]

These were extremely trying times for Zumpt personally and for the country. In April 1917, the United States entered World War I.[12] The following month Congress approved the Conscription Act of 1917 (commonly referred to as the Selective Service Act), which required all men, ages twenty-one to thirty, to register with their local draft boards. It was the first selective service army raised in the United States.[13]

At twenty-seven years of age, Zumpt was required to register. Draft registration day was 5 June throughout the country. By the end of that day, 19,214 Atlanta men had registered. It was reported in the local paper that only one man in this age group failed to report. Each man who registered was assigned a draft number, and the first in a series of drawings of draft numbers from this pool of registrants took place on 20 July, in Washington, DC. All men who were assigned the numbers that were drawn were required to report to their local exemption boards for physical examinations in order to determine their fitness for military service.[14]

There is no indication that Zumpt's draft number was drawn so that he would have been required to report. If his number had been drawn, he would have been eligible to apply for a deferment. Under the Selective Service Act, deferments from service could be applied for and were granted for a number of reasons, one of which was for men with economic dependents.[15] With a wife, child, and other family members dependent on him for their sole financial support, Zumpt would have been granted an exemption. Whether Zumpt's number was drawn or not, he did not serve in the United States military during World War I.

Of the draft-eligible male population in the United States, only 20 percent served in the military during World War I.[16] Zumpt was part of the 80 percent who did not serve. Atlanta sent a total of 7,890 men into service during this war. This number included volunteers as well as draftees.[17]

As World War I was drawing to a close, Zumpt and Roberta had their second and last child. On 23 September 1918, another daughter, Mildred Ballenger Huff, was born.[18] Happy times continued for Zumpt and Roberta two months later with the celebration of the signing of an armistice with Germany on 11 November 1918, bringing an end to the fighting in World War I.[19]

Over the succeeding years, Zumpt continued moving his family around Atlanta and continued working as an electrician. In 1925, Zumpt and Roberta were living in southeast Atlanta on Clarke Street,[20] and by 1926 they were living in southwest Atlanta on Stewart Avenue. That year also marked a change in his occupation. According to the *Atlanta City Directory*, in 1926, Zumpt was working as the manager of Capitol View Filling Station.[21]

The year 1926 marked the last year that Zumpt lived in Atlanta and the state of Georgia. He moved his family to Orlando, Florida, where he returned to working in movie theaters. In Orlando, Zumpt operated the Colony Theater. He also worked at the Baby Grand Theater in nearby Winter Park. The family lived in Orlando in an apartment above the theater. Recalling those days, Roberta said they could put an ear on the floor of the apartment and listen to the movie playing below. Zumpt also lived for a while in Titusville, Florida, and then moved to St. Petersburg in 1933, where he switched occupations again. He returned to working as a journeyman electrician.[22]

Zumpt remained in St. Petersburg until the outbreak of World War II. At the time of the Japanese attack on Pearl Harbor, 7 December 1941, Zumpt was fifty-two years of age and too old to be eligible for the military draft. Instead, he decided to contribute to the war effort by moving to Jacksonville, Florida, in 1942, where he worked on rewiring the Jacksonville Naval Air Station. It was during these years that Zumpt's thick, black hair turned solid white.[23]

For decades Zumpt had been a heavy smoker, and he developed a bad case of asthma. As World War II was ending, his physician told him that he had to quit smoking or he wouldn't live much longer. This dire prognosis had a profound effect on Zumpt. He quit smoking that very day and never smoked again.[24]

While in Jacksonville, as he had done since first leaving his father's home, Zumpt rented the residences where he and his family lived. But in 1960, now approaching seventy-one years of age, and with both of his daughters having married and moved out, Zumpt decided it was time that he and Roberta owned their own home. He built a one-story, cinderblock home on 6th Avenue North in Jacksonville Beach, Florida. Zumpt did most of the work on the home himself, which included installing all of the wiring, outlets, and electrical box in the home. It would be the home Zumpt would live in for the rest of his life.[25]

After settling down to a family lifestyle, Zumpt became an avid reader and continued this interest into his later years. It was not uncommon for him to be awake in the early hours of the morning still reading the book he'd started earlier in the evening. According to a granddaughter, Zumpt read every Western novel that author Louis L'Amour wrote.[26]

Zumpt and Roberta also spent many hours listening to music, especially opera and classical music. Zumpt owned an extensive collection of records that he played on his old Victrola wind-up phonograph player, which he converted into an electric record player.[27]

Every job that Zumpt had during his life involved working with his hands. As he advanced in age, he developed arthritis in both hands. The electrical wiring work he did in Jacksonville required nimble fingers. As his arthritis grew steadily worse, he tried every remedy he came across, medical remedies and old home remedies alike, in order to be able to continue working. He sometimes rubbed turpentine into the joints of his fingers to relieve his arthritis pain. When that didn't work, he rubbed kerosene into his joints, and on other occasions he would try rubbing with olive oil. He even tried acupuncture once, with some success. But he lamented that acupuncture treatments were too expensive to keep up. Despite his arthritis Zumpt continued annually to renew his Jacksonville business license to work as a journeyman electrician.[28]

After becoming a resident of the state of Florida, Zumpt rarely thought of his involvement in the Epps-Huff partnership. Only occasionally would he speak of the days he and Ben built and flew the first airplane in Georgia. When he did, it was only with family. His last documented visit to Athens, Georgia, occurred in April 1917 when his father's body was brought to Bernstein Brothers Chapel for preparation and then burial in Carnesville next to Annabel. But as Zumpt approached the eighth decade of his life, that would change.

In summer 1968, the *Atlanta Journal & Constitution Magazine* ran a story on Ben Epps, Jr., and the replica airplane that he'd built of his father's 1912 monoplane (the Epps VIII Monoplane).[29] Ben Jr. was living in Atlanta and working as a pilot with Southern Airways at the time. Zumpt had three sisters and a number of nephews and nieces living in Georgia when the article appeared. One of these family members cut the article out and mailed it to Zumpt.

Bringing a flood of memories, the article prompted Zumpt to contact Ben Jr., although he'd never before met or communicated with him before. As a result of this contact, Ben Jr. invited Zumpt to Atlanta to see the replica 1912 monoplane. He also told Zumpt that he had his father's scrapbook with photographs of the early planes that his father had built. Zumpt made arrangements to travel to Atlanta that fall.

Zumpt was thrilled to be able to meet Ben Jr. upon his arrival in Atlanta and was impressed with the job he'd done building the replica plane. The replica was kept in a hangar at Epps Aviation, which was owned by Ben Jr.'s youngest brother, Pat Epps. The aviation service business was located at DeKalb Peachtree Airport in Atlanta, where Ben Jr. was able to demonstrate the replica plane's flying abilities for Zumpt.[30] But the highlight of Zumpt's trip was seeing the photographs in Ben Sr.'s scrapbook. He'd not seen the pre-1911 photographs of the early planes built by the Epps-Huff partnership since shortly after the photographs had been developed, almost sixty years ago. He had no idea these photographs were still in existence.

Zumpt asked for copies of some of the photographs, and Ben Jr. agreed to provide them. Arrangements were made to send the originals of the photographs Zumpt wanted to a company in Massachusetts that could take the originals and make negatives and copies. A bill for some of these copies, addressed to Zumpt, from Smithway Studios, West Somerville, Massachusetts, dated 17 December 1968, is part of the Benjamin Thomas Epps Papers at the Hargrett Rare Book and Manuscript Library at the University of Georgia in Athens.[31]

Not long after Zumpt's visit to Atlanta and subsequent return to Florida, he was contacted by Ben Jr. and invited to attend a presentation that he was giving to the Athens Historical Society on "Ben Epps Night." The event was being held on 9 January 1969, in Athens.[32] Zumpt was excited about going to the meeting so he could hear Ben Jr.'s presentation on building the replica of his father's 1912 monoplane and his father's achievements in the field of aviation. He made arrangements to meet Ben Jr. in Atlanta, and together they flew to Athens.

At the historical society's meeting, Ben Jr. introduced Zumpt to the group as a "friend" of Ben Sr.'s. Near the end of Ben Jr.'s presentation, one of the attendees asked Zumpt to offer his impressions and remembrances of Ben Sr. Zumpt spoke of his admiration of Ben Sr. and provided the group with a few anecdotes of the efforts to get the early planes to fly. He spoke only of Ben Sr. and said nothing about himself or his role in building the first planes. When the floor was opened to questions, someone asked when in 1907 Ben Sr. made his first successful flight. Like others who had tried to recall specifics about this flight decades later, Zumpt could not remember the date. Ben Jr. was also unable to provide the exact date, only that it was thought to have taken place in 1907. Zumpt did recall and offered to the group that a newspaper reporter had been present and wrote an article detailing the specifics of the first flight.

The next day, while Zumpt was still in Athens, he went to the Clarke County Courthouse, where the old editions of the *Athens Banner* were stored, and searched for the article about the first flight. And, like those before him who'd searched for the 1907 article, Zumpt, too, was unable to find it.

Several days later, after Zumpt had returned to Jacksonville Beach, the president of the Athens Historical Society, Richard N. Fickett, III, wrote to Zumpt, thanking him for attending the meeting and asking,

> Did you find the copies of the Athens newspagers [*sic*] you were looking for in the court house [*sic*] here[?] I plan on getting over there in a few weeks and searching more for the newspaper articles of the flights, etc. (Last month I looked through spring of 1907 papers, without success).[33]

Bob Fort, a newspaper reporter in Athens, was also in attendance at the meeting of the Athens Historical Society in January 1969. He wrote an article ten days later that appeared in the *Athens Banner-Herald & Daily News*, captioned, "Athens' Ben Epps—Pioneer Aviator of the South." For the first time since 1909, the name "Zumpt Huff" was mentioned in print in connection with Ben Epps's first flight.

Fort identified Zumpt as someone who "worked closely" with Ben Sr. and described his impressions of Zumpt as being a man who "combines a sharp mind with a short wit to underscore the true color of 'the old days.'"[34] Fort was not the only one Zumpt impressed at the Athens Historical Society meeting. The society's president, who'd written to Zumpt, also sent a letter to Ben Jr. to thank him for his presentation and for bringing Zumpt. Fickett commented in his letter to Ben Jr. that Zumpt was "remarkable for his age, has a remarkable memory, and can certainly talk."[35]

The focus of Fort's article was Ben Epps, Sr. He did not delve into the extent of Zumpt's role in building and flying the first planes in Georgia. Even if Fort had asked about the extent of his involvement, Zumpt, as part of his nature, would have downplayed his role. This would have been particularly true on a night billed as "Ben Epps Night." Zumpt would have thoroughly enjoyed hearing the praise heaped on his old friend and former partner. He would not have thought twice about being relegated to a role of one who had only "worked closely" with Ben Sr.

As a result, Fort did not grasp the significance of the role Zumpt played in the first flight and wasn't able to appreciate the depth of his involvement. An opportunity was missed that night in Athens to correct and expand on the historical record. But Fort did pick up on the fact that Zumpt "worked closely with Ben Epps in Athens when the pioneer was building and flying the very first airplanes in the State of Georgia and the Southeast."[36]

Ironically, this Athens Historical Society meeting was held in the year that marked the sixtieth anniversary of the first flight. Yet no one at the meeting realized this fact, not even Zumpt, who returned to Florida without receiving the credit he was due. Unfortunately, this was the last time Zumpt was in Athens.

Zumpt Huff was seventy-nine years old when he attended that meeting of the Athens Historical Society. If he was ever going to record the history of the first flight in Georgia and tell the story of the Epps-Huff partnership, now was the time. After giving the matter some thought, Zumpt decided to make a wood-framed, glass collage of photographs of the planes that the Epps-Huff partnership built. The frame, according to Zumpt, would be about twenty-four inches by thirty-six inches. He wrote to Ben Jr. in February 1969 and described additional photographs in the scrapbook that he would like to have copied. There were to be five photographs in the frame, plus another five photographs for the other projects Zumpt was working on. Each photograph added to the collage would be accompanied by a caption, which Zumpt would author, providing an historical narrative of what the photograph depicted and the role that particular plane played in the design developments of the Epps-Huff partnership.[37]

In addition to the collage that he was making for himself, Zumpt had an ambitious plan to make five more of these wood-framed collages with the intent of donating one each at planned ceremonial presentations to the University of Georgia Library, the Athens Historical Society, and the Hayden Burns Library of Jacksonville, Florida. He was also giving one to Ben Jr., with the fifth collage going to Ben Jr.'s brothers and sisters to share.

Zumpt also contacted the editor of a local magazine in Jacksonville about carrying the story and publishing some of the photographs.[38] Finally, Zumpt had thoughts of publishing a book about the Epps-Huff partnership and its accomplishments. At the time he was formulating these ambitious projects, he had no references to jog his memory of the details of the work of the Epps-Huff partnership. Other than the few photographs he was having copied, there were no books, no articles, no letters, no notes, nor anything else available to help reconstruct the facts and chronology of events that would properly reflect the history of the Epps-Huff partnership. For the first time in many decades, Zumpt was piecing together memories of events that had taken place sixty years earlier. But before he could complete the history and these projects, there was one piece of information he needed, but could not recall—the exact date of the first flight.

Zumpt's search of the newspapers at the Clarke County Courthouse while he was in Athens had not provided the answer. The day after the president of the Athens Historical Society wrote his "thank you" letter to Zumpt, Fickett went back to the courthouse to search further for the date of the first flight. During this search, Fickett found the 14 May 1909 article in the *Athens Weekly Banner* entitled, "Two Athens Boys Building Airship." This was the article about the building of the biplane, the Epps-Huff I. Fickett had the article copied and mailed it to Zumpt.[39] From this article Zumpt now knew the correct year that the first flight took place: 1909.

Zumpt wrote to Ben Jr. a month later asking for help following up with the photography company that was making copies of the photographs from Ben Sr.'s scrapbook that were to be used in the collages, the proposed magazine article, and Zumpt's future book. The letter also follows up on a request Zumpt made to Ben Jr. for additional photographs to be copied:

> I hate to keep bothering you about these photo's [*sic*], but I need them very much [*sic*] I will list them for you again, I will need one of Ben, on Page 8-D of the Atlanta Journal [*sic*] July 7th, 1968, and the one of you on the front page.
> In the Athens Banner Magazine [*sic*] Jan 19th, 69 [*sic*], in the upper top left hand corner of Page 8-D, and one of your Dad on the same page. I need a copy of the one you have of the Wreck [*sic*] at Lynwood Park, this one is the only one I have seen that you have of the Plane he made his first and second flight in, within [*sic*] 24 hours.[40]

In the first paragraph quoted above it's clear that Zumpt still has in his possession the copy of John Pennington's article that appeared in the *Atlanta Journal & Constitution Magazine* on 7 July 1968, which was mailed to Zumpt by one his family members living in Georgia and which started this whole process of Zumpt documenting the story of the Epps-Huff partnership. The last sentence of the second paragraph is the closest documentation that exists of Zumpt confirming the fact that there was a private, nighttime flight prior to the public, daytime flight: "the Plane he made his first and second flight in, within [*sic*] 24 hours."

Zumpt's 21 February 1969 letter also informs Ben Jr.,

> I believe I am on the right track now to get the exact data [*sic*] of that first Flight, I need this to back my statement up. When I get the above I will complete my book, and will have it readied for publication.[41]

In April 1969, Zumpt was still trying to secure the copies of the photographs he needed for his projects.[42] Eventually, he received some, but not all of the ten photographs that he wanted copied. However, almost a year later he was still searching for the date of the first flight, which he had to have before he could complete his projects. In February 1970, Zumpt mailed Ben Jr. a photograph of a former coworker of his and Ben Sr.'s at Morton & Taylor Electrical, Julius D. Baker. On the back of this photograph Zumpt typed, in part,

> I believe I have located a news paper [*sic*] that has the story of the 1st Flight with the date, Will go up and search their files, as soon as I can get away. I have gone over a lot of search [*sic*] for this since last I saw you.[43]

Zumpt subsequently wrote in the scrapbook he put together for himself that the first flight occurred on "August 31, 1909."[44] He provided no explanation in his scrapbook, or anywhere else, as to how he arrived at this date. The first flight did not take place on 31 August 1909 (it was actually conducted on 28 August 1909), but this was the date that the *Atlanta Constitution* featured a front-page article about the second attempt at flight. It's not known whether Zumpt ever saw this article, or the first article that appeared in the *Atlanta Constitution* the day before (30 August 1909), since there were no copies of either of these articles in his scrapbook or framed collage. But with what Zumpt thought was the correct date of the first flight, he was ready to complete his projects.

Zumpt put five of the reproduced photographs in a handmade wood frame, approximately twenty-four inches by thirty-six inches, under glass. One of the photographs was a portrait of Ben Sr. The other four were photographs of airplanes built by the Epps-Huff partnership: Epps-Huff I Biplane, Epps-Huff II Monoplane, Epps-Huff III Monoplane, and Epps-Huff V Monoplane. (Zumpt's notes never mention the Epps-Huff IV Monoplane, which was completed in December 1909 and was the last model monoplane before the partnership switched to a Blériot-inspired design.)

Zumpt typed narratives on each of the four airplane photographs, and below three of these photographs, he typed a further narrative on a short sheet of paper. He also added a lengthy narrative on the back of the quintessential photograph of Ben and the Epps-Huff II Monoplane in front of the garage on East Washington Street. The narrative on the back of this photograph is both typed and handwritten in pencil and appears to be two different drafts of the narrative. When this photograph was attached to the collage, the narrative on the back was hidden from view.[45]

One of Zumpt's framed collages was in the possession of his youngest daughter, Mildred Huff Laughlin, until her death in Ohio, in April 2010, and is now in the possession of her daughter, Zumpt's granddaughter, Teresa Laughlin Gensheimer.[46] This is the only framed collage made by Zumpt that is known to exist. The former Hayden Burns Library is now part of the Jacksonville, Florida, Public library system, which has an extensive collection of photographs of Florida residents and their historical accomplishments. But this library does not have a photograph collage made by Zumpt.[47] Neither is there such a collage in the collections of the Hargrett Rare Book and Manuscript Library at the University of Georgia in Athens, nor one in the possession of the Athens Historical Society.

Zumpt did not get around to publishing a book about the Epps-Huff partnership. It would have been difficult for Zumpt to have typed a lengthy narrative for publication, but he apparently did record his narrative on tape, which a third party could have transcribed. Zumpt referred to such a tape on the back of the photograph of Julius D. Baker, which was mailed to Ben Jr. in February 1970. Zumpt typed to Ben Jr.,

> I have 1/4" tape recording 400-feet, I would like to send you, if you can get some one, to copy it on a tape for your record, if you will send me the original back.[48]

Zumpt is referring to a tape that could be played on a reel-to-reel tape recorder. High-speed reel-to-reel recorders were the main recording format used by audiophiles and professional recording studios from the 1960s until the late 1980s. It is not known what happened to Zumpt's tape. It was not located in his scrapbook or collage, and none of Zumpt's living descendants know of the existence of such a tape. To be able to hear the narrative of the Epps-Huff partnership in Zumpt's voice would have been an historic treasure.

Other than the notes in his scrapbook and the captions and narrative accompanying the photographs in the collage, there is no written historical account of the first flight penned by Zumpt. Correspondence from Zumpt to Ben Jr. makes reference to Zumpt having contacted a local magazine editor to do an article on the Epps-Huff planes and Ben's first flight, but no copy of an article of this type was found in Zumpt's possessions at the time of his death. A nephew of Zumpt's did recall having received from his uncle an article about

Zumpt, Ben, and the first flight that appeared in a Jacksonville newspaper magazine, which had a color drawing of a plane on the cover. But according to Thora O. Kimsey's *Our Family Tree, Ficquett-Wilbanks-Huff, Extended Families, 1788–1995*, this nephew no longer had the article at the time that this family history was published in 1995. Efforts have been made to locate this magazine article but have not been successful.[49]

On 1 October 1971, at eighty-two years of age, Zumpt renewed his city of Jacksonville "Journeyman Electrician" license for the last time. Zumpt died four years later in Jacksonville, on 23 November 1975. He was survived by his wife, Roberta, two married daughters, Katherine and Mildred, five grandchildren, eleven great-grand-children, and four of his sisters.[50]

Benjamin T. Epps, Sr.:
The Post-Partnership Years 1911 to 1923

After Zumpt moved and the partnership dissolved, Ben concentrated on settling into his new garage and working on a new design for a monoplane. But 1911 held an even bigger change in Ben's life, one that would ultimately become the most profound. That was the year when Ben met Lucille Omie Williams.

Omie was born in Neese, Madison County, Georgia, on 17 February 1894, the youngest of five children of William B. Williams and Eliza Adeline Eberhardt Williams. There were almost eight years difference between Omie and the next youngest child.[1] Omie was twelve when her father sold the family farm in Madison County and purchased another farm in Greene County, Georgia, where land was cheaper. The family moved to a home in the small village of Siloam.[2]

At age sixteen, Omie wrote to Michael Brothers, the largest wholesale and retail dry goods store in Northeast Georgia, located in Athens, and asked for a job. One of her brothers was working in Athens at the time with Athens Railway and Electric Company. Omie was invited to come for an interview, and a few days after that interview was offered a job. The job paid fifteen dollars a month and resulted in her parents moving with her to Athens. Although the family moved from Siloam, her father continued to manage his farm and sawmill near that village and commuted back and forth.[3]

At the time of her move to Athens, Omie was engaged to be married to a young man who was studying at Clemson University in South Carolina to become a Presbyterian minister. When her fiancée heard about her proposed move, he strongly disapproved of her living in Athens. He expressed a prescient fear that she would meet someone there who she liked better and call off their engagement. But Omie told him not to worry; she was too involved with her music to meet anyone else and too deeply in love with him for that to ever happen.[4]

It's been said about life that desire sets our compass, but real life steers our course. Shortly after starting work at Michael Brothers, Omie was leaving the store one day on her way to lunch. She saw a boy she knew and stopped to speak to him, and as they talked, Ben Epps came walking down the sidewalk. The boy Omie was talking to was a friend of Ben's, so Ben came over to say hello to his friend and introduced himself to Omie.

Omie was familiar with Ben's name, as was everyone who lived in and around Athens. She knew he was the airplane inventor and that his garage was conveniently located one block over, around the corner from Michael Brothers's East Clayton Street store.

The casual meeting on the street did not end there. For some time afterward, the boy who'd introduced her to Ben kept asking Omie if she would like to go on a date—automobile riding at night. But Omie was engaged to someone else and refused to consider a date. However, her friend's persistence paid off. Omie finally relented and agreed to ask her mother if it would be all right. To Omie's amazement, her mother consented to her going on the nighttime automobile outing, as long as another couple went with them.

On the night of their date, Omie's friend surprised her. She walked out of the door of her parents's house to find Ben and another girl in the backseat of the automobile, acting as the "other couple." But a bigger surprise awaited: Omie was caught completely off guard when her friend informed her, as they reached the automobile, that he was *not* going to be her date for the evening after all. She would not be riding up front, but in the backseat: Ben was to be her date.

Omie quickly made sure Ben was aware of the ground rules. This was not really a "date," it was an outing among friends. After all, she told Ben up front, "I'm engaged to be married." But Omie's pronounced "already spoken-for" status made no difference to Ben. He confidently boasted to her later that evening that he "was going to beat her fiancée's time."[5]

Starting that night, Omie learned that Ben possessed an amazingly strong resolve. He refused to give an inch in his pursuit of her. Ben had his mind made up that one day he was going to ask for her hand in marriage. Despite her protests that she was engaged and that she was only interested in friendship, Ben was confident he would eventually win her over.

Omie and Ben first appeared together on the society page of the local paper on 10 September 1912. They were listed as guests who attended a "charming party" at the Claud Whatley home on Doughtery Street.[6] Omie and Ben made the society page again, one year later, when they "motored" together with Ben's sister, Ruth, and others to Toccoa for a day outing.[7]

Ben demonstrated to Omie his resolve again and again during the two years that they dated. He was certain her armor was showing signs of a crack, and it was growing. Finally, Omie could protest no more. She relented to Ben's prodding and said "yes" when he popped the question. On 7 December 1913, Omie and Ben were married in Athens.[8] They moved in with Ben's parents and his nine siblings, who were still living at 1020 West Hancock Avenue. After Ben had dropped out of Georgia Tech, his parents had three more children, who were three, six, and eight years old when Ben and Omie moved in.[9] The newlyweds lived there for the first two years of their marriage.[10] But before they moved out, the house would become even more crowded.

On 6 October 1914, Ben and Omie had their first child, a daughter, Evelyn. It didn't take long for Evelyn to make the society page of the paper herself. Fewer than two months after her birth, the paper thought readers would be interested in learning that the young aviator's wife had taken their seven-week-old daughter to Siloam to visit Omie's parents, who'd moved back to Oglethorpe County.[11] During these years, Ben continued to design and build airplanes. Omie recalled in an interview years later that Ben showed the same, never-ending perseverance when "he started to build airplanes and wouldn't quit," as he did while they dated.[12] In that 1939 interview, Omie also confirmed that Ben's first flight was "a short flight in 1909"[13] and that he continued to design and build airplanes from the time they met throughout most of their marriage. Airplanes were part of his being.

When Ben began his pursuit of Omie, he'd finished building and was testing his 1911 monoplane, the Epps VII, an improved version of the Epps-Huff V and Epps-Huff VI, based on the Blériot design. He redesigned the fuselage of the Epps VII from a square-shaped frame to a triangular frame. Also, the two bicycle wheels under the tail section were removed and a short skid added in their place to keep the tail off the ground. Like the previous model, a single skid was centered between the front two wheels. The performance of the Epps VII was an improvement over the two previous models. The altitude, distance flown, and control were all better, but all three models were restricted to straight-line flights due to control problems when turns were attempted. A big step toward correcting this problem occurred in Ben's design for his 1912 monoplane, the Epps VIII.

Every plane model that Ben had been involved in designing up to this point used wing warping as the means of attempting to control the plane's flight. But with the 1912 Epps VIII Monoplane, Ben abandoned the wing warping method in favor of using ailerons. The word "aileron" is French for "little wing."[14] Ailerons are hinged flight control surfaces attached to the trailing (back) edge of the wing of a fixed-wing aircraft. They are used to control the aircraft in roll, which results in a change in heading due to the tilting of the lift vector. The two ailerons are typically interconnected so that one goes down when the other goes up. The down-moving aileron increases the lift on its wing while the up-moving aileron reduces the lift on its wing, producing a rolling movement about the aircraft's longitudinal axis.[15]

The aileron came into widespread use around 1915, well after the rudder and elevator controls.[16] The Wright brothers used wing warping instead of ailerons for roll control and initially, their aircraft had much better control in the air than aircraft that used movable surfaces. However, as aileron designs were refined and aircraft became larger and heavier, it became clear that ailerons were much more effective and practical.

There are conflicting claims over who first invented the aileron. English inventor Matthew Piers Watt Boulton patented the first aileron-type device for lateral control via "flexed" wings in 1868. But his patent was forgotten until the aileron was in general use.[17]

Although Boulton described and patented ailerons in 1868, no one had actually built them until Esnault-Pelterie's glider, almost 40 years later.[18] Henry Farman's ailerons on the Farman III were the first to resemble ailerons on modern aircraft and have a reasonable claim as the ancestor of the modern aileron. In 1908, Glenn Curtiss, as a member of the Canadian aeronautical research group, Aerial Experiment Association, flew an aileron-controlled aircraft, the "White Wing." Curtiss subsequently dropped out of the A.E.A. and, to the dismay of that group, patented their aileron invention and reportedly sold it to the U.S. government.[19]

In addition to adding ailerons, the wings of Ben's 1912 Epps VIII were covered with fabric on the top and bottom. The fuselage was triangular-shaped with a tapering empennage (the tail assembly) and two landing wheels.[20] With this model, Ben returned to using two skids, which were positioned on the inside of the landing wheels. For more power he installed a 35-horsepower engine.[21] Another addition to the 1912 Epps VIII was an alarm clock. The alarm clock served as a safety feature to time fuel consumption and warn the pilot when the fuel tank was getting low. This plane design proved to be the best performing to date.

There were no new models in 1913. A good portion of Ben's time during this year was spent pursuing Omie, becoming engaged, and then planning for his December 1913 marriage. But Ben was always about building a better plane model, and the following year his creative mind went back to work on a new one.

According to handwritten notations in his scrapbook, Ben built another plane "about 1914 using fuselage of the 1912 monoplane."[22] The design of this plane was similar to the 1912 Epps VIII with the exception of the wing tips. Instead of the traditional rounded wing tips that Ben had used in his previous three designs, with this model he experimented in cutting off the trailing edge of the wing tips. The wing-tip shape influences the wing-tip size and the drag of wing-tip vortices. There are four photographs of the Epps IX Monoplane on a single page of Ben's scrapbook showing the testing of the new wing-tip design in the field.[23] Although the notes on this page say that the plane was built "about 1914," it may be that this model was not built until 1915. There are no planes depicted in Bens' scrapbook for 1915, but the *Athens Banner* reported in August 1915 on the crash of Ben's "new" airplane: on 25 August 1915, "while Mr. Ben Epps was making a trial flight of his new aeroplane, the machine was wrecked pretty badly, but the operator was in no way injured. His clear head and prompt action saved him."[24] This latest crash prompted Ben to contemplate yet another design for a plane that would be rolled out the following year.

The Epps X was a second biplane design. But unlike the first biplane, this one incorporated ailerons instead of using wing warping to control roll. By spring, the 1916 Epps X Biplane was ready for a public appearance.

In May 1916, the *Athens Banner* sponsored an auto show in Athens. The show was held in the city auditorium. It began on Tuesday, 23 May, and continued through Saturday. Ben, as an agent for automobile manufacturers, exhibited autos and his newly built biplane.[25] An article promoting the show proclaimed, "Without a doubt one of the most interesting displays at the show will be the flying machine put on exhibition by Mr. Epps who has manufactured one right here in Athens and made a number of flights with it."[26]

But Ben's second biplane did not last long. On its seventh flight, the Epps X Biplane crashed, ending up nose-down in a field. It was never rebuilt.[27] After designing and building ten different models of airplanes, and with the recent birth of a second child, his first son, Ben took a break from designing and building planes.

Ben and Omie became parents again when Ben Jr. was born on 27 June 1916.[28] Living arrangements at Thomas J. Epps's home were cramped, to say the least; Ben and Omie needed their own home to raise their children. Ben's father thought so, too, and in January 1917, he gave Ben two acres of land in Clarke County on the road from Athens to Epps Bridge, a half mile from the city limit of Athens.[29] The property was about 200 yards east of Thomas Epps's small country store. At the time of this gift, the corporate limit of Athens was a distance of two miles in every direction from the center of the University of Georgia chapel.[30] This property was in a rural area and considered far from downtown. It was located on a section of the present-day Old Epps Bridge Road, west of Hawthorne Avenue, in the curve of Old Epps Bridge Road into the Atlanta Highway. Now that Ben was a landowner, he went to work building a new home for his family.

Omie described the new home as a "nice house...with a well on the back porch and kerosene lamps, with a nice garden, chickens, cows and...a hog or two."[31] It had a two-car garage with a cement floor. Ben installed a thirty-two volt light plant in the garage so they could have lights in the house at night. Ben Jr. recalled years later,

> It was my job every afternoon to start the Delco engine generator to charge the batteries.... After the light plant had been installed Daddy installed a water pump. The pump was about four

feet high and had an electric motor on top that was connected to the pump by a chain drive that made about as much noise as a small motorcycle when it was running. All in all it was a good system—especially at a time when nobody—but nobody, had running water in the country.[32]

Another modern convenience Ben added to his country house was a telephone. There was no telephone line available along Epps Bridge Road, so telephone service was not available at the new home. To have telephone service, Ben ran his own line from the house and connected it himself to the telephone line inside the city limit. As the only house in this rural area to have a telephone, neighbors would come to Ben's house when they needed to make a call.[33]

The house and garage sat on one acre, and on the other acre Ben built a cow lot, pigpen, chicken yard, and two vegetable gardens. He also planted peach trees, plum trees, fig trees, muscadine vines, and a strawberry patch. His daughter, Evelyn, would milk the cow at night by the light of a lantern and read a book at the same time. Ben Jr. milked the cow on occasion, but his primary job with respect to the animals was to feed the cow and chickens, slop the hogs, and clean the cow lot.[34]

As Ben, Omie, and their two children settled into their new home, the United States entered World War I in April 1917. Under the terms of the Conscription Act of 1917 (the Selective Service Act), all men, ages twenty-one to thirty, were required to register with their local draft boards, on 5 June 1917, to be called for service.

Clarke County registered 1,500 men from which its full quota of 181 men was to be selected for service.[35] Ben, his brother, Carl, and a cousin went together to the courthouse in Athens and registered. Each registrant was assigned a draft number. Ben's number was 254, Carl's 255, and their cousin's 256.[36] The numbers of the men to be drafted were randomly selected during a series of national drawings.

The first drawing took place in Washington, D.C., on the morning of 20 July 1917. With a blindfold covering his eyes,

Secretary of War Newton Baker drew the first number from a large glass jar and read it out: 2-5-8.[37] As Ben heard the first two numerals called, he must have realized that the chances of his number being drawn had suddenly increased dramatically. There were a mere four numbers between Ben's number and the one that was selected. After each drawing, the names of those selected were published in the Athens paper. Ben's number was never drawn.[38]

Deferments could be applied for and granted to men with economic dependents.[39] With a wife and two small children, Ben would have been eligible for a deferment had he been drafted. Although Ben did not serve in the military in World War I, his brothers Carl and Roy did.[40]

With the uncertainty of whether he would be serving in the military behind him, Ben focused on a new project. Before the year concluded, he entered into an agreement with the Clarke County Board of Commissioners to lease a tract of land from the county about three miles outside of the Athens city limit. On this land Ben built the first civilian airport in the state of Georgia.[41] Atlanta would not have an airfield for another two years.[42] This site is the location of today's Athens-Clarke County-Ben Epps Airport. From this location Ben offered plane rides, aerial photography, and flying lessons.

With so many men involved in fighting the war in Europe, economic times in the United States were tough. It was becoming harder and harder to collect on bills, even in the garage business. In February 1918, the garage and automobile dealers in Athens took out an ad to notify the public that beginning on 15 February, each of their places of business, which included Epps Garage, was going on a "spot cash"-only basis, requiring customers to pay cash for all services before their automobiles would be released.[43]

Nine months later an armistice was signed and World War I came to an end.

The end of the war brought a surplus of planes available to purchase. There was no need to build a plane when one of these surplus planes could be purchased for less than it cost to build one. Ben bought several of these planes, reconditioned them, and sold them, becoming the state's first used-airplane dealer.[44]

In spring 1919, there was one surplus plane for sale in particular that captured Ben's eye. It was owned by the naval department of the U.S. government and located in Springlake, New York. It was an Aeromarine 40, a two-seat seaplane trainer aircraft that was a real novelty, and which Omie referred to as the "flying boat."[45] The Aeromarine Plane and Motor Company of Keyport, New Jersey, manufactured the plane. It had an eight-cylinder, 135-horsepower, Thomas-Morse designed engine. In 1918, the United States Navy ordered 200 Aeromarine 40s, but with the end of World War I in November of that year, production was cut back to only fifty.[46]

Without Omie's knowledge, Ben had been able to set some money aside from his garage business, his flight lessons, and the charters he was offering at the new flying field. He came across an advertisement for the Aeromarine and was intrigued. It needed some work, but Ben saw an opportunity to fix it up, resell it, and make good money. He traveled to New York, purchased the flying boat, and had it shipped to Athens. After doing some reconditioning work, the plane was ready and Ben advertised it for sale.

A young Englishman, Louis Montague "Monte" Rolfe, responded to the ad. Monte was born in London and moved with his parents to the United States before the outbreak of World War I in Europe. Monte became a famed aviation pioneer, dubbed the "boy aviator."[47] He learned to fly in 1915 at the Curtiss Seaplane School in Newport News, Virginia, which had been founded by Glenn Curtiss. Monte had developed quite a reputation touring the states flying at state fairs. He claimed to have flown in every state.[48]

Monte told Ben he was selling the Aeromarine plane too cheap and offered some ideas on how even more money could be made on the flying boat. Ben invited Monte to Athens during summer 1919, where the two worked together for three weeks on the plane until it was ready to be put back on the market. Omie recalled that Ben advertised it for the price of $100,000.[49] The flying boat attracted the interest of a group of potential buyers in New Jersey, so Ben and Monte flew it there to demonstrate its capabilities for this group.

Monte was at the controls during one such demonstration when he was forced to make an emergency landing. He put the plane down on a small area surrounded by trees. After making repairs, the plane was ready for takeoff. Unfortunately, the area where Monte was attempting the take off was too small to achieve enough speed to clear the trees. The plane clipped the treetops and crashed. Although the plane was badly damaged, no one was seriously hurt. But the dream of a high-priced sale and a big profit was over.[50]

Ben and Monte brought the damaged flying boat back to Athens by train and went to work converting it into a land plane. It was "especially constructed for the purpose of carrying passengers" and was "arranged with every detail adding to the comfort."[51] Their plan was to charge people for a ride in the plane and hopefully recoup some of their investment.

The local paper announced that Monte and Ben were forming an air-taxi service that was offering joyrides in the clouds over Athens beginning in October. The service would have two planes, the one in Epps Garage being converted and a second on order from the Naval Department that was being shipped and was somewhere between New York and Athens. The air-taxi service would consist of hauling passengers, flight-school work, and aerial advertising, but the primary service was to be fifteen-minute joyrides for a price of $10 each.[52]

At the time that Ben and Monte were setting up their air-taxi service, Atlanta resident James H. Elliott was clearing and leveling a 3.5-acre area of the old Atlanta Speedway near Hapeville to be used as an airfield. In 1909, Asa G. Candler, Jr., son of the Coca-Cola Company magnate, had formed a group of investors to purchase 300 acres south of Atlanta, near Hapeville, and built a lavish automobile racetrack patterned after the Indianapolis Speedway. But due to poor revenues, the speedway closed after its first season. Over the succeeding years, the raceway hosted a few air shows and races and occasionally was used by pilots barnstorming in planes.

In 1919, Candler leased the property to Elliott, who built Atlanta's first civilian airfield on the property. Elliott operated his flying business on this property until 1923. It wasn't until 1925 that Candler leased the property to the city of Atlanta for a term of five years to be used as a municipal airport. The Atlanta City Council named the airfield Candler Field after the Candler family, in hopes that Asa Jr. would eventually donate the property to the city. But Asa Jr. was not as prolific a philanthropist as his father; in 1929, the city of Atlanta purchased the property from Asa Jr. for $94,500.[53]

Ben was asked about the possibility that his new air-taxi service would offer trips to Atlanta. He estimated that a trip of that distance could not be made for less than $125, which was a lot of money in 1919. There were not enough people willing or able to pay that price to support regular air service between Athens and Atlanta. But Ben was quick to add that if a person were willing to pay for such a trip, it would be arranged.[54]

Ben and Monte became close friends. They formed the Rolfe-Epps Flying Company in fall 1919, which they incorporated in Clarke County the following summer. The company's office was located in Epps Garage on East Washington Street. The stated purposes of the company were "conducting a school of flying, carrying passengers in aeroplanes, doing exhibition flying; advertising; buying, and selling, repairing and manufacturing aeroplanes and aeroplane motors, gas and gasoline engines...buying, leasing, holding or renting landing fields...and to do all other things incident to the business of flying."[55]

Although there were a few cities in the South that had an airplane sales company, Athens was thought to be the first to have a company formed for the purpose of carrying passengers on airplanes, as well as offering advertising from the air. Besides the comfort built into the Rolfe-Epps Flying Company airplanes, passengers did not have to wear a "monkey-suit." This was considered to be "quite a feature to the conventional person, who would hesitate long in changing the 'conventional calico' for the trousers of the 'movie avion.'" Passengers also did not have to wear goggles, since a wind guard protected their eyes.[56]

Around the time that Rolfe-Epps Flying Company was being formed, Monte moved his wife and two-year-old daughter to Athens.[57] Monte was introduced to the residents of Athens as a twenty-five-year-old pioneer aviator who had been flying since 1910. (According to his brother, Doug Percy Rolfe, Monte started flying in 1915).[58] He'd flown in no fewer than twenty states and was a member of the famous Coventry Aeroplane Society of England. Besides being a pilot, Monte was an "expert aeroplane designer and is recognized as an authority on the testing of [airplanes], he being one of the few aviators in the country whose official endorsement will be taken by the companies insuring aeroplanes."[59]

Business for the Rolfe-Epps Flying Company was good from the start. When Ben and Monte flew over the streets of Athens on 20 November 1919, dropping advertising circulars for their business, calls started pouring in to Epps Garage to schedule a flight. By that evening, several hundred requests had been received. Flights were made daily.[60]

With the start of a new year, the company announced that it would be sponsoring a "Big Day at the Aviation Field!" to be held on Sunday, 8 February 1920. From 10:00 A.M. until dark, flights over Athens, Crawford, Winterville, and regular joyrides were offered at prices from $10 to $25 dollars.[61] It promised to be a "thrilling" aerial exhibition. Monte had secured a man for the show who would "do all the latest tricks while in mid air, such as walking out on the airplane wings, standing on his head while the 'ship' is moving at the rate of

90 miles an hour, hanging by his head and feet from the machine and other modern dare-devil acts." The person Monte had secured to perform these daredevil acts was Lt. Roscoe Turner, formerly with one of the United States Army Balloon Squadrons in France during the war.[62]

According to Monte, Lt. Turner was one of only three men in the United States who was doing acrobatic stunts in the air. And, not too surprising, Lt. Turner was said to be the only man on record to have ever hung from a plane by means of a rope around his neck.[63]

That same month, another aviation "first" was witnessed in Athens. For the first time, the *Athens Banner* was delivered by airplane to Elberton and Washington, Georgia, and advertising circulars for the newspaper were dropped from the air, all distributed by the Rolfe-Epps Flying Company.[64] The enterprise, which now touted ownership of three planes, also began offering aerial photography. To demonstrate the company's capabilities, Monte flew over the downtown business section of Athens, the residential and suburban areas, manufacturing plants, and schools and college buildings, taking photographs, which were then put on display for the public to view.[65] Some of the photographs that Monte took on that occasion are part of the collection of the Benjamin Thomas Epps Papers, Hargrett Rare Book and Manuscript Library, University of Georgia Libraries, Athens, Georgia.[66]

The following March, another "dare-devil" came to Athens to put on a stunt-flying show. The H. W. Campbell United Shows featured "sensational stunt flying" by Monte and Dare Devil Holder. The show promised to "outdo all previous aerial exhibitions as to sensational flying and wing walking." The performance at the Lexington Road field concluded with a parachute drop and landing on the show grounds.[67]

As the field of aviation continued its rapid growth, Ben and Monte envisioned airfields popping up all around the state. They knew that the passing of an airplane overhead would become common in sections of the state where planes were seldom seen. Both men were interested in promoting this growth and visited nearby towns looking for suitable landing sites to develop. Monte was reported in February as being in Winder, Georgia, looking for a site for a landing field.[68]

In August 1920, Rolfe-Epps Flying Company put on a month-long promotion with the Athens Apperson automobile company. Everyone coming in to test drive a new Apperson automobile received a free airplane ride in one of the Rolfe-Epps Flying Company's airplanes. The promotional slogan in the ad stated, "Next to a Spin in an Apperson a Trip in a Curtis [*sic*] Plane." The first flight was scheduled to take place on Monday, 2 August, and the ad copy alerted readers to "watch for the big Curtis [*sic*] Plane carrying a satisfied owner of an APPERSON.... Drive an APPERSON FIRST then experience the next most wonderful sensation—A Dip in the big CURTISS PLANE."[69]

By the end of the year, the Rolf-Epps Flying Company was no longer doing business. It's not clear what caused the company to dissolve, but Monte began a new venture by January 1921. The *Lenoir* (NC) *News-Topic* reported that Monte and Lt. Harry Runser, who piloted the first airplane to cross the Blue Ridge Mountains, were establishing a plant to manufacture airplanes in Marion, North Carolina. The name of the new company was Marion Aircraft Corporation, which would build the "Carolina Cloudster," a commercial plane they hoped to build entirely from North Carolina products, except for the motor. The facility would make Marion the first city in the South to boast a plant that manufactured airplanes from the ground up.[70]

This North Carolina venture was the first of a series of brief jobs that Monte took after leaving Athens. From Marion, Monte went to work with the Augusta Aircraft Company, in Augusta, Georgia, and by summer 1921, he was in Havana, Cuba, piloting planes for the Cuban American Aerial Transportation Company.[71]

Ben and Monte continued to stay in touch by exchanging letters. Monte wrote to Ben from Cuba on 10 August 1921 in response to a recent letter he'd received from Ben in which Ben had enclosed a photograph of the midget motorcar he'd built for Ben Jr. Monte's reply letter described his latest job. Business was slow and his employer owed him $500. He mentioned that his wife and daughter had recently left Cuba to go take care of her sick mother.

Monte was apparently feeling a little homesick. He said he wanted to come back to the States just to be around people who spoke English. He invited Ben to come join him in Cuba, although he said he couldn't afford to pay him. He tried to lure Ben by suggesting he come see all the beautiful Cuban women, but then acknowledged that Ben was happily married and wouldn't be interested in other women.[72] Sadly, before Ben received Monte's letter in Athens, Monte was killed when the plane he was flying in Havana broke apart in midair and crashed. He was survived by his wife and three-year-old daughter.[73]

Monte's younger brother, Lt. Douglas Percy Rolfe, of St. Paul, Minnesota, sent a letter to the editor of the *Athens Banner-Herald* advising the paper of his brother's untimely death and asking that an article be placed in the Athens paper so that Monte's many friends in Athens could be informed of his death and his funeral service being held in Evansville, Indiana.[74]

By the start of January 1922, Rolfe-Epps Flying Company became Epps Flying Company and Captain A. G. Davis, a former aerial serviceman, replaced Monte Rolfe. That same month, Ben purchased a new plane. The plane was to be used for commercial purposes and piloted by Davis. Ben was optimistic that his airfield on Lexington Road would be used as a stopping point on the anticipated New York-to-Atlanta airmail route, which was in the planning stages.[75]

To house the new plane, Ben secured permission from the Clarke County commissioners to build a hangar at the airfield. Since leasing this property from the county, he'd been using a large canvas tent stretched over poles as a hangar. The tent was taken down and stored in the basement of Ben's house on Epps Bridge Road.[76] The Lexington Road airfield now had its first permanent hangar. The future Candler Field would not be leased to the city of Atlanta until April 1925 and did not have its first permanent hangar until late 1926 or early 1927; coincidentally, this hangar would be built by a man who would soon be joining Ben in Athens.[77]

Ben and A. G. Davis continued to give flying lessons, offer rides, and perform aerial stunts. By summer 1922, another ex-serviceman arrived in Athens and began working with Ben. The new acquaintance was Doug H. Davis.[78]

Doug dropped out of high school in Barnesville, Georgia, and volunteered with the U.S Army Air Service in 1917 as the United States was entering World War I. He was commissioned at seventeen years old, making him one of the youngest, if not the youngest, pilot in the service. Doug was discharged in 1919 and organized a group to barnstorm New York City and surrounding areas. He came south to Athens in 1922 and joined Ben putting on flying shows and performing stunts. He brought with him his IN-4 yellow "Jenny," which he kept at Epps Field.[79] In addition to his plane, Doug brought to Athens a new wrinkle to air shows for the amusement of the Southern crowds.

Doug owned a fox terrier named "Mexican Dynamite," who would hang around Epps Garage and at the flying field. Dynamite's role in the air shows was to parachute from the stunt planes. The dog was said to be "no happier than when gliding peacefully over the city, at a height of about a thousand feet...[and] just adores the parachute glide." On occasion Dynamite even "hopped out of the plane at a height of several thousand feet with a tiny parachute strapped about him, to float down to the ground."[80]

Dynamite's parachuting feats made an obvious impression on a young Ben Jr. When he was old enough to participate in barnstorming over Northeast Georgia with his father in the 1930s, he had his own parachuting dog that was part of the air show.[81]

Doug did not remain in Athens for long, but it was long enough for him to establish a close bond with Ben. Doug subsequently merged his air show with the Cody Flying Circus, which was run by Mabel Cody, a niece of Buffalo Bill Cody's. Together they spent 1923 performing primarily in Florida. In 1924, Doug formed a unit of the Baby Ruth Flying Circus to advertise the new candy bar that had been recently introduced. He then returned to Atlanta and was instrumental, along with Beeler Blevins, in convincing the mayor of Atlanta, Walter A. Sims, and alderman, William B. Hartsfield, that Atlanta needed to be involved in the age of aviation. Doug and Beeler urged the city to lease the old Atlanta Speedway and develop it as a municipal airfield. Doug went on to build the first permanent airplane hangar on Candler Field, inside the racetrack near the old home-stretch area. He also formed Doug Davis Flying Service, a school of aviation.[82]

Fair week came to Athens in October 1922, and Ben signed up to be a part of the entertainment. He contracted with the fair committee to make daily flights over the city during the week to promote the fair and performed "sensational aerial stunts" over the fair buildings at different hours of the day.[83]

During this year Ben was appointed by the Clarke County commissioners to serve on a committee tasked with making a recommendation as to whether the airfield should be designated as a field on the official route of the Aircraft Association of America. At a December 1922 meeting of the board of commissioners, Ben presented the committee's findings, recommending that the airfield be designated as part of the official route. In support of this recommendation Ben pointed to the significant growth in the commercial aviation business all across the nation and explained that this designation would serve to promote Athens by advertising throughout the country that a landing field was available there. He predicted this would result in many planes coming to Athens and probably some Army dirigibles, too, since the route was to eventually be taken over by the U.S. government. The commissioners agreed and adopted Ben's recommendation. Since the field that Ben was using was too small to meet the requirements of the Aircraft Association of America, the commissioners also voted to enlarge the field.[84]

As part of the enlargement project, Ben explained at the meeting that the Aircraft Association of America worked in conjunction with the Boy Scouts of America. Local Boy Scout troops would have the job of preparing the runway markings on the field. The markings would be made of rocks or cobblestones, which the scouts would whitewash frequently so they could more easily be seen from the air and located by pilots on their maps.[85]

The Lexington Road airfield was considered by the Aircraft Association to be ideally located. It was "but three miles from the city on a paved road and near the county farm, which affords telephones and other accommodations needed while the hangar owned now by Mr. Epps will afford shelter for an additional plane.... The elevation is 700 feet."[86]

While working on this county committee, Ben also served on a city committee to bring airmail service to Athens. It was announced early that year that it was possible that Athens would be a stopping point on the New York-to-Atlanta airmail route, which was to be established soon.[87] Mayor George C. Thomas appointed an Air Board for the city in an effort to have Athens put on another proposed air route. This route was from Washington to New Orleans. Ben was asked to serve on this committee and represented the commercial aviation interest. He served along with his brother Carl, who represented the American Legion.[88]

The city of Atlanta was also vying for a place on the United States airmail routes. Atlanta's Air Board was busy putting together an airfield with the assistance of Asa Candler, Jr., to meet the requirements of the U.S. Post Office.[89]

Despite the efforts of the Atlanta Air Board, Atlanta did not have regular airmail service until 15 September 1926.[90] Thanks in part to Ben's groundwork, Athens, too, was placed on the U.S. airmail service route in 1949.[91]

The recognition and "firsts" that Ben brought to Athens through his aviation endeavors seemed unending. The following year he would accomplish yet another "first" while flying his plane.

Saturday, 10 November 1923, was a beautiful day in Athens. There wasn't a cloud in the sky and the fall air was "a bit nippish."[92] Some 10,000 visitors had descended on Athens for homecoming at the university. Noted Athenian Dan Magill described it as "one of Athens' most eventful days and perhaps the most successful of the University's 'Homecoming' celebrations."[93] The sidewalks were crowded with the colors of red and black, interspersed with the combination of blue and orange. The Georgia Bulldogs were set to play the University of Virginia Cavaliers in a football game at 3:00 P.M. on Sanford Field.[94]

Just over two miles east of Sanford Field, Ben was at the airfield meeting with Francis E. Price, a staff photographer for the *Atlanta Constitution*. Ben had purchased another plane in January. It was in the new hangar at Epps Field when a terrific wind and rainstorm tore through the area in March. The high winds had completely destroyed the hangar, which fell on Ben's Curtiss plane and caused hundreds of dollars of damage. The timing was bad. It was the start of spring and good weather, when the patronage of Epps Flying Company picked up significantly. It took weeks to repair the damage to the hangar and Curtiss airplane, but both were now fully repaired and Price was ready to go flying with Ben.[95]

Ben had agreed to fly Price over Sanford Field while the game was in progress so he could take photographs from overhead. The result of Price's work was published in the Sunday edition of the

Atlanta Constitution, on 25 November 1923. It was the first aerial photograph of a college football game in the state of Georgia, a precursor of the blimps that now appear regularly in the sky above sporting events transmitting aerial footage.

The photograph was taken "during a tense moment of the Georgia-Virginia game" and was described as "remarkably clear [in] every detail of this unusually good airplane photograph.... Even the action of the players and the antics of the cheer-leaders register perfectly."[96] An accompanying photograph of Ben seated in his plane with Price standing next to the plane dubbed Price as the "Flying Photographer."[97] Clinging to a 6–0 lead midway through the fourth quarter, a Virginia miscue led to a Georgia touchdown and a 13–0 win of its homecoming game.[98]

Ben was impressed with how Francis Price had taken the concept of flight and applied it in a way that took his profession to another level, figuratively and literally. Ben, too, wanted to apply aviation in a new way to his design work. He'd not built a new design since his 1916 Epps X Biplane, but he'd never stopped thinking of new concepts. Now he wanted a design that would not only be novel, but would have a similar impact on aviation as Price's groundbreaking work had on photography. He thought he could achieve that goal if he could conceive a design that would make his life's passion, aviation, accessible to a vastly larger group.

It wasn't long before Ben had the idea he was looking for, and he was certain it would be a game changer.

11

Achievements and Agony

There were no new designs or planes built by Ben from 1917 to 1923, primarily because of the surplus of military planes available at that time. But in 1921, Ben designed and built a two-seat, midget motorcar. It was referred to as a "unique little 'automobilette'" that was four feet high and eight feet long. It was powered by a four-cylinder motor and was reported in 1930 as being able to travel as fast as seventy miles an hour. It was a fun, sporty-looking car that was simple to operate and easy to maneuver, and it could be seen, on occasion, speeding through the streets of Athens,[1] Ben Jr. and his older sister, Evelyn, took turns driving the midget car around the yard. This was the same midget car in the photograph that Ben mailed with his letter to Monte Rolfe in Cuba.

Another attribute of the midget car was the fact that it was not expensive to make. It could be built for far less than the cost of a new car. Ben was proud of his work on this vehicle, and the car gave Ben an innovative idea. He began to think about designing and building a monoplane for the average person that could be affordable and easy to fly, the same attributes of his midget car. Ben's latest project to go from dream to reality was unveiled when he rolled out his 1924 Light Monoplane—a midget monoplane, the Epps XI.

The 1924 Epps XI Light Monoplane weighed only 350 pounds, had a wingspan of twenty-five feet, and was powered by a two-cylinder Indian motorcycle engine. It could travel twenty-five miles on a single gallon of gas and reach an air speed of sixty miles per hour. It cost about $750 to build, and Ben thought the cost could be lowered if the plane was mass-produced.[2]

For more than a year, Ben worked on this plane in his shop and experimented with it at the flying field trying to produce a practical airplane that would offer the lowest cost and maintenance possible. He hoped to reduce the weight to 300 pounds, increase the speed to seventy miles per hour, and achieve sixty to seventy miles distance per gallon of gas. It was designed for commuting to towns where landings and takeoffs were accomplished in extremely small areas, and it was predicted that when this plane was perfected, it would be "one of the outstanding developments in aviation of this decade."[3] Ben's work on this plane brought him national attention, and he received correspondence regarding this plane from all over the country.[4]

The local press dubbed Ben's latest model the "midget plane."[5] The Epps XI Light Monoplane was demonstrated for the public at the flying field on 30 May 1925, which was noted as the fourth successful flight of the "midget plane."[6]

Despite Ben's efforts to sell his new concept, financial success remained elusive. Ben was not able to attract investors or generate the capital he needed to turn his 1924 Epps XI Light Monoplane into a commercial enterprise in which the plane could be mass-produced.

The frustration and disappointment weighed on him. Feeling like he was losing a family pet, Ben was forced to sell his midget plane. He placed an ad in the paper and it was ultimately sold for $1,000. This amount wasn't much more than his out-of-pocket expenses to build the plane and was no compensation for the untold number of hours spent to develop it.[7]

One can only speculate how different Ben's life would have been if he'd been able to commercially produce and sell his 1924 Epps XI Light Monoplane. Had he done so, it might have resulted in the construction of a large airplane manufacturing facility in Clarke County and produced unimaginable wealth for Ben and his family.

Seven years later, another pioneer aviator exemplified what life might have been like for Ben if he'd been able to commercialize the production of this plane. The 1924 Epps XI Light Monoplane turned out to be a precursor to the 1931 Cub aircraft built by William T. Piper, Sr., of Lock Haven, Pennsylvania. Like Ben, Piper had the idea to build an airplane that people would find easy to buy and easy to fly. The Piper Cub was the result. The plane was immensely successful and served as the "nursery for hundreds of thousands of pilots."[8] With the success of the Piper Cub, William T. Piper became known as the "Henry Ford of Aviation."[9] From an initial investment of $400, over a period of thirty years, he amassed a family fortune estimated at more than $30,000,000.[10]

The excitement and sense of pride of accomplishing yet another plane design with the 1924 Epps XI Light Monoplane, arguably the most innovative and successful yet, along with dreams of mass-producing this plane faded quickly for Ben when tragedy struck just days after the 31 May 1925 public demonstration of the new plane.

Ben was at the airfield late on Thursday, 4 June 1925. He was busy making money giving flight lessons and plane rides over the surrounding area. A Winder High School student, Otis "Burr" Camp, Jr., who'd just finished his junior year and was on summer break, had driven to the Lexington Road airfield with two friends to go on a plane ride. Each had his turn in the plane with Ben.

Burr was taking his turn and sitting in the front seat, and Ben was seated behind him handling the controls. They'd just passed over downtown Athens on their return to the airfield. Ben was lining up the Curtiss model plane for a landing.[11] It was about 7:30 P.M., and the plane was in a slow descent, seventy-five to one hundred feet in the air.

Suddenly, the plane went into a tailspin. Burr's two friends looked on in horror as the plane fell from the sky and struck nose-first into an embankment on the Winterville Road, the road from Lexington Road to the airfield. His friends raced to the crash site along with a number of University of Georgia student pilots who were at the airfield. They were joined by a contingent of prisoners who came from the nearby county prison farm to help.[12]

Because he was seated in front, Burr absorbed the brunt of the impact. He was wedged between the gas tank and parts of the plane from the rear, which crushed him in a vice. The only way his rescuers could extract him was from the underside of the fuselage.

Burr was rushed to St. Mary's Hospital where he was pronounced dead a short time later as the result of a fractured skull. He was only seventeen years old and considered one of the best prep athletes in North Georgia, having played both football and baseball. He was the third son of the Barrow County sheriff, Otis Camp, Sr.[13] Burr's hometown newspaper said he was "one of the brightest and most popular boys in this city and his tragic death has cast a gloom over the entire city."[14]

A section of the plane struck Ben across his face causing a nasty gash and severe bruising. His right leg was also badly injured. It was feared that his spine was fractured, too, at the base of his skull. Ben was rushed to Athens General Hospital, and initially his injuries were thought to be so serious that it was reported, "Little hope is felt for his recovery."[15] His condition as of 3:00 P.M. the following day was reported as,

> a fracture at the base of the brain. Just how serious this is cannot yet be determined. He has talked intermittently, in a broken manner, from time to time but is not aware of what happened to him.... He has a lacerated leg, a broken wrist and a badly cut and bruised face in addition to the shock he received. He is bleeding from one ear, also.[16]

Burr's funeral took place in Winder on Sunday. With his parents' consent and as an expression of sympathy, Athens pilots provided a plane that flew over the interment ceremony at Rose Hill Cemetery and dropped flowers onto Burr's grave. A University of Georgia student who had just completed a course of training under Ben was picked to drop the flowers from the plane.[17]

On the following Monday, the subheading in a follow-up article said Ben's situation was still serious, but there was some improvement as "Ben Epps Shows Steady Gain in Fight for Life."[18] It would be a long, slow recovery process.

The physical recovery was difficult, but not nearly as difficult as his emotional recovery, which was longer and more painful. Ben had children, too, and as all parents know, to lose one is the most difficult experience imaginable. But despite the physical pain and mental anguish, Ben's first plane crash involving a death didn't taint his love for flying or alter his belief that an airplane was safe and would become the preferred mode of long-distance travel by the public in the future. Flying was a passion he would instill in his children.

Since moving into the house on Epps Bridge Road, the size of Ben and Omie's family had expanded significantly. With the start of 1929, they now had six children with a seventh on the way.[19] Four were in school and those who were not soon would be. Living in the country was becoming ever more problematic for Omie, who had to get the children to school in Athens and back home again. When she was not able to pick them up, one of the workers at Ben's garage would be sent to bring them home.

Omie was also active in the children's school lives and in the Parent-Teacher Association, which significantly increased the number of trips she had to make to Athens. (Her commitment to the PTA would later result in her being honored with a lifetime membership in the National Parent-Teacher Association.) She told Ben they were living too far out and needed to move into the city. It was a conversation they had several times over the years, but Ben was not receptive to moving.[20]

Ben was again enjoying good health and his garage business was doing well. He was making money from flying lessons, plane rides, and aerial photography mixed with the occasional sale of a reconditioned plane. Omie decided it was time to approach Ben again about moving into the city. She told him "it was too expensive to send so many [children] to school in town."[21] This time Ben relented, but he added an admonition, "All right, but as sure as we do, one of the children will be killed sure."[22]

Acquiescing to Omie's request, in 1929 Ben bought a lot inside the city limit of Athens. It was Lot 11, Block 1 of Lynwood Park.[23] It was no coincidence that Ben chose this lot to build on. The lot was on Hill Street, the high ground of Lynwood Park, where on 28 August 1909, Ben took off in the Epps-Huff III. The lot was designated as 892 Hill Street[24] and provided the best view down The Plaza, the approximate flight path of the Epps-Huff III, although The Plaza did not exist as a street in 1909; it wasn't built until later.

According to a daughter, Ben traded a car for this lot.[25] He built a home and, after the birth of his son, William Douglas Epps, on 9 March 1929, moved his family into the new residence. It was a red brick house with a lattice fence that screened the backyard, where the garage was located.[26]

That same year was the twentieth anniversary of the first airplane flight in Georgia. The occasion did not go unnoticed in Athens. The *Athens Banner-Herald* reminded its readers of the anniversary of that historic event in its 4 August 1929 edition but without mention of the specific date in August 1909 when the flight occurred.[27]

There was time for one more accomplishment before the 1920s came to a close. But Ben did not achieve this accomplishment; instead, it was Ben Jr.'s turn to make a mark on the field of aviation.

12

Georgia's Aviation Family

The year 1929 marked the twentieth anniversary of the first flight in Georgia. That year was also a milestone for Ben's family for another reason as well. Ben Jr. started flying with his father when he was ten years old, and a year later Ben began giving his son lessons at the controls of the plane.

Ben Jr. was anxious to learn to fly and showed an amazing propensity for mastering his lessons. But his father knew the dangers inherent in flying, even among experienced and well-trained pilots. Ben also knew what Omie would think if she learned that he was showing Ben Jr. how to operate the controls, so the lessons were few and far between. However, beginning in early spring 1929, the lessons took on a different tone. Both the frequency and intensity changed dramatically. The experience that Ben had developed over years of training himself and others to fly, he now patiently and meticulously conveyed to his son.

Ben had recently bought a Waco 9, which he considered an excellent plane for Ben Jr. to learn how to fly.[1] The plane was purchased from his former associate and good friend Doug Davis, who was working as district manager of Southern Air Transport out of Candler Field in Atlanta.

Since leaving Athens, Doug had become an avid participant in airplane races. In 1926, Ben joined Doug in his plane in an air race from Atlanta to Philadelphia. They made the first leg to Greenville, North Carolina, at a speed of 100 miles per hour and were contenders for a top prize. But the next day bad weather forced their plane down in Danville, Virginia. Ben decided to return to Athens while Doug flew on to Philadelphia and finished the race.[2] They also worked together later in 1926 to plan a performance by the Cody Flying Circus in Athens, although inclement weather forced the cancellation of the performance.[3]

Many times Doug tried to talk Ben into moving to Atlanta and coming to work with him at Candler Field, but Ben's roots were firmly entrenched in Athens and he never seriously considered moving.[4] His children's favorite memories of Doug Davis were associated with his bringing them Baby Ruth candy bars every time he came to Athens to visit. In his early days of barnstorming, Doug was part of the Baby Ruth Flying Circus. One of his stunts, particularly when flying over Coney Island, New York, was dropping Baby Ruths attached to small parachutes.[5] Ben and Doug's relationship was so close that when Ben and Omie had their seventh child in March 1929, they named him William Douglas Epps after Doug Davis.

Ben Jr. turned thirteen years old on 27 June 1929. A freshman at Athens High School, he weighed only 100 pounds and was five feet tall but was "strong and wiry." He had "dark brown hair and wide-awake, interested-looking gray eyes."[6] He also had his father's perseverance and was focused on learning to fly.

On Sunday afternoon, 20 September 1929, Ben and his family were at Epps Flying Field watching planes take off and land. This was how the family spent Sunday afternoons after church service. As the day was drawing to a close, Omie took the children home to start dinner, except for Ben Jr., who wanted to ride home later with his father. Now that mother was not around, father and son decided to take the Waco 9 up for a lesson.

Ben Jr. wrote his remembrances of that day decades later:

> After shooting about 4 or 5 landings Daddy turned around in his seat and asked me if I thought I could make it around the field by myself. I figured I could so he got out and I taxied down to the end of the runway—opened the throttle and took off. I flew

around the field and made a perfect landing. While on the down wind leg I was thinking, "Now I've got it up I've got to get it down." I think Daddy was real proud of me.[7]

That evening, when the family was seated around the dinner table, Ben and Ben Jr. could not stop grinning. Omie knew something was up and wanted to be let in on the secret. When she was told that Ben Jr. had soloed, "she almost fainted."[8]

At only thirteen years old, Ben Jr. was the youngest person in the country to fly solo.[9] Thanks to a proud father, word of Ben Jr.'s solo flight spread. It also helped that his solo flight was in a plane bought from Doug Davis. Doug had become a well-known aviator through national air races. He had just broken world speed records in the National Air Races in Cleveland and had won the coveted Thompson Trophy. Doug was preparing for the upcoming Atlanta Air Races, a two-day event scheduled to begin 9 November 1929. After hearing of Ben Jr.'s solo flight, Doug made arrangements to invite Ben Jr. to the Atlanta races to demonstrate his flying abilities.[10]

As excited as a child on Christmas morning, Ben Jr. prepared for his demonstration at Candler Field by making daily flights over Athens. He attended both days of the races in Atlanta and flew his father's Waco 9 solo, making several laps around the field. He "handled the plane perfectly."[11] It was the first time Omie saw her son fly solo and she commented that "he handled it just like his daddy." But years later Omie was more reflective. She told an interviewer, "When I look at these children of thirteen it frightens me to think of the things we let him [Ben Jr.] do."[12]

Ben Jr. was not the only child of Ben and Omie to earn aviation accolades at the end of the 1920s. Not many months after Ben Jr. made history with his solo flight, his older sister, Evelyn, decided she wanted to take flying lessons, too. Evelyn was fifteen years old when her father started teaching her to fly. At that time she was the youngest female in the state of Georgia to take flying lessons.[13] Ben and Omie's two oldest children established a family tradition that their younger siblings anxiously voiced they wanted to follow. The Epps family was unlike any other in the state, and that fact did not go unrecognized.

Valco Lyle, a journalist on the staff of the *Athens Banner-Herald*, dubbed the Eppses "Georgia's Aviation Family" in a July 1930 article published in the Sunday *Atlanta Constitution Magazine*. The article detailed the aviation accomplishments of Ben Sr., Ben Jr., and Evelyn and featured the quintessential photograph of the Epps-Huff II, along with a photograph of all three in front of the Waco 9. The article went on to point out that there were five other children in the family, four boys and a girl. Ben told Lyle that the other children would also be learning to fly, as soon as they "acquire enough aviation knowledge and physical strength to manage a plane."[14]

Next in line to learn was eleven-year-old Mary Virginia. Virginia was described as restlessly waiting her turn to take lessons and intended to learn at an even younger age than her sister, Evelyn. Even the baby, fourteen-month-old William Douglas, had been up in his father's plane sitting on his mother's lap. He laughed and enjoyed his ride before falling asleep, according to his mother. Asked about the future direction of aviation, Ben told Lyle that the transportation of light freight by plane would be common in the near future, but "I don't believe...that it will ever be practical to carry heavy freight by airplane."[15] Even a pioneer aviator and visionary such as Ben could not fathom the power and flying capabilities of today's airplanes.

Subsequent to the publication of this article, Valco Lyle prepared a condensed version that he sent, along with the same two photographs, to the Associated Press Feature Service. The Associated Press sent the article layout to hundreds of their subscribing newspapers all over the country, and the resulting national exposure brought even more accolades to "Georgia's Aviation Family."

Shortly after the Associated Press story ran, nationally renowned radio news reporter and commentator Floyd Gibbons selected the Epps family for one of his topics on his evening radio show. Gibbons first gained fame as a war correspondent for the *Chicago Tribune* during World War I. As a result of valor on the field of battle, he received France's greatest honor, the Croix de Guerre with Palm. In the 1920s and 1930s, he was widely known as a radio commentator and narrator of newsreels, famous for his fast talking delivery. Using the Associated Press story, Gibbons told his evening radio audience of the flying proclivities of the Epps family.[16] Ben was listening to Gibbons's radio program that night, and by letter dated 26 September 1930 told Gibbons how much he appreciated the kind words Gibbons spoke about his family.[17]

The national broadcast of "The Flying Family of Georgia" by Floyd Gibbons brought still more accolades. Ben Jr.'s solo flight accomplishment caught the attention of Edith "Jack" Stearns Gray. Jack was a pioneer barnstormer herself, flying with her husband, Captain George A. Gray. They passed through Georgia several times between 1910 and 1914. She knew many of the early aviators and was writing a history of American aviation when she learned of Ben Jr.'s solo flight. Her book, entitled *UP, A True Story of Aviation*, was scheduled to be published on 1 November 1930.

After hearing Floyd Gibbons's radio broadcast, Jack wrote to Ben Jr. telling him about her upcoming book and asking him to send her pictures of himself, his plane, and his pilot's license. She also said she wanted to include a short chapter on him and his solo flight in her book. Ben Jr. sent the pictures requested and thanked her for including him in the book. He told her he liked the title and was "anxious to see it."[18]

Jack's book, *UP*, was published in 1931 with a chapter about Ben Jr. and his solo flight. She called him a "wonder boy!" and "a veritable juvenile [Charles] Lindberg."[19]

In June 1931, Ben Jr. traveled to Washington, D.C., with a friend and his friend's family. While there, he decided on his own to contact Jack at her home in Chevy Chase, Maryland, and made arrangements to meet with her. Ben Jr. wrote to his parents from

Washington, D.C., to tell them that he'd gone to see Jack and that she'd invited him and his friend out for dinner. He also told them that Jack had arranged an appointment for him to meet President Herbert Hoover at the White House at noon the following day, 4 June 1931.[20] Ben Jr. was able to speak personally with President Hoover in the White House for about five minutes and made the papers again.[21]

After Ben Jr. returned to Athens, Jack wrote to Ben and Omie to tell them what a fine son they'd raised. She went on to say, "During my nineteen years of close association with aeronautics I have met many celebrities of aviation—both pioneer and modern, but none have I been more honored to know than your very wonderful boy flyer."[22] She also wrote to Ben Jr. and gave him some sage advice: "Be careful and don't stunt."[23]

In the years that followed, Ben Jr. teamed up with his father flying at fairs around the state. They became popular "barnstorming" stars over North Georgia flying stunts, contrary to Jack's admonishment, and competing in air races. One of the stunts they reinstituted was the parachuting dog, a throwback to Ben's days of working with Doug Davis and his parachuting fox terrier, "Mexican Dynamite."

This time the disinclined star of the show was "Bob," a small, brown rat terrier. Ben Jr. made Bob's parachute and harness. The event was advertised in the paper and promoted by Ben Sr. and Ben Jr. flying over Athens at about 200 feet dropping circulars detailing all the stunts that would be performed at Epps Field.

A large crowd was on hand to see Bob's first performance. When Bob refused to jump, he was gently dropped and performed flawlessly. The show became a regular Sunday afternoon event. Bob went on to make a total of nine jumps before deciding that he'd had enough and disappeared, never to be seen again. Despite the loss of Bob, Ben Sr. and Ben Jr. continued to barnstorm, which helped pay for the gas and maintenance of Ben's airplanes.[24]

Ben Jr. went on to have a distinguished flying career. During World War II he served as a flight instructor in the United States Army Air Corps and flew numerous missions from India to China over "The Hump," carrying fuel to aircraft based in China. "The Hump" was a route over the mountains in that region and was considered extremely dangerous. After the war, Ben Jr. became a commercial pilot, retiring from Southern Airways in 1976 as a captain. Like his father, he, too, was inducted into the Georgia Aviation Hall of Fame (1994).[25]

During World War II, Evelyn and Virginia used what they'd learned from their father about flying at the U.S. Naval School in Atlanta, where for three years they taught men how to fly in ground-based simulators.[26] Sons James Harry and Charles Whitfield also flew in World War II and were licensed pilots. Ben's next two sons, George Frederick and William Douglas, similarly became licensed pilots. Doug Epps became a career pilot with Delta airlines.[27]

Ben's youngest son, Ernest Patrick, who was born 23 February 1934, not only became a licensed pilot, but made a career in aviation. He has been the owner and operator of Epps Aviation at DeKalb-Peachtree Airport in Atlanta since 1965. Like his father and oldest brother before him, Pat Epps was also inducted into the Georgia Aviation Hall of Fame. He was a 2011 inductee.[28] Only the youngest child, Rosemond Claire (Sissy) Epps, born 29 March 1935, never learned to fly.

All the accolades that Georgia's Aviation Family received were wonderful. But life is never all joy. Tragedy visited the Epps family, too, and often.

13

The 1930s: Years of Tragedy

During winter 1930, Ben spent a good deal of his time in his garage on East Washington Street building a new biplane. It would turn out to be his last airplane design. This model, the 1930 Epps XII, was a light biplane, which he called the "Eaglerock." It's not clear why he chose this moniker. But perhaps it was related to Ben's knowledge of a certain plane model that was popular with barnstormers. The Alexander Aircraft Corporation, based in Denver, had been building a biplane it called the Alexander Eaglerock since 1925. From 1928 to 1929, Alexander Aircraft was the largest aircraft manufacturer in the world, but financial problems hit and the company liquidated in the early 1930s.[1]

Ben had previously built a light monoplane, the 1924 Epps XI, and his new design was a biplane version of that concept. The 1930 Epps XII Light Biplane looked like an Alexander Eaglerock but was much lighter. It was an improved version of the 1924 Epps XI Light Monoplane. Instead of a two-cylinder motorcycle engine, the Epps XII was powered by a Ford Model A engine, making it Ben's first and only plane with a Ford engine.[2] It had a wingspan of twenty-eight feet, while the Alexander Eaglerock had a wingspan of thirty-six feet and weighed a hefty1,420 pounds.[3]

By June 1930, Ben was testing the new plane.[4] It performed well, but he was determined to improve its performance even more. The following year he replaced the Ford engine on the Epps XII with a 90-horsepower de Havilland Gipsy motor, made in England. With the new engine installed, in February 1931 Ben eclipsed the air speed record from Atlanta to Athens by a local flyer. Piloting the Epps XII,

Ben was able to make the trip in forty-five minutes. The 1930 Epps XII Light Biplane could fly at a maximum speed of 110 miles per hour.[5]

The following month Ben went for a second record while piloting his new plane in the skies over Athens. On 19 March 1931, he set the altitude record for aviation in Athens when he reached a height of 12,600 feet, which was 2,040 feet higher than two miles. The long-standing previous record had been set by Ben's friend and former partner, Doug Davis, when he reached a height of 8,000 feet. It took Ben thirty minutes from takeoff to reach the record-setting height, but only ten minutes to make the descent. The plane and new motor, he said, "performed perfectly."[6] It was a feat Ben accomplished just five days after the death of his brother Roy, who was only thirty-four years old.[7]

The 1930 Epps XII Light Biplane caught the attention of *Popular Aviation*, a national aviation magazine published in Chicago. In a three-page article, the Epps XII was praised for its low construction cost and attractive style. The author of the article recommended this plane for the "amateur who would like to build his own plane." The article was illustrated with pictures of the Epps XII, drawings that detailed the dimensions and weight of each part and showed how the plane was constructed.[8]

Ben built this plane with the intention of commercially producing and marketing his design. But once again, the economy throttled his plans. He told the author of this article, "Just about the time flight tests were completed, the well-known depression had become such a serious matter that marketing plans were abandoned."[9]

Ben's flight instruction school was also at its peak in the early 1930s. The cost of learning to fly was now affordable for most people. Ben advertised his classes at a cost of $10 per lesson or $200 for the full course. He noted in some of these advertisements that even Charles Lindberg had to be taught to fly.[10]

Learning to fly and becoming a licensed pilot had become wildly popular in Athens. This "call to the skies" was answered by people from vocations across a broad spectrum. "Students, women, salesmen, lawyers, professors, grocerymen, mechanics, engineers and chemists [were] learning to become pilots at the Athens airport."[11] One of Ben's students became the first woman to solo in Athens, Clarice Miller of Columbus, Georgia. While a junior at the university, she took lessons almost every day for a period of weeks before making her solo flight.[12]

Ben took a special interest in each student he taught. The process of going through flight school promoted bonding, and with the issuance of a pilot's license, the student became part of a unique "brotherhood." Ben's scrapbook reflects the contact he maintained over the years with a number of his students. He felt a sense of pride in what these students accomplished in the field of aviation, knowing that he helped make their achievements possible. But Ben would never have acknowledged publicly that he played any role.

In 1931, there were two flight schools at the airport in Athens. One had twelve students, who were taught by M. C. Armel, a pilot who'd logged 400 to 500 hours of flight time. The other school was Ben's, which boasted sixteen students. Their teacher had built up 3,000 hours of flight time.[13]

Not everyone who took lessons from Ben, however, mastered the art of flying. There was a crash at the airfield in September 1928 involving a student pilot. Ben was in the front seat and his student pilot in the backseat, operating the stick. The student was attempting to take off when the plane suddenly swerved off the runway and hit several parked automobiles. The automobiles were damaged and the wings of the plane were smashed, but Ben and his student escaped serious injury.[14] Such were the risks of training student pilots.

One of Ben's students in the class of 1931 was Ed Hamilton. Ed was a resident of Athens and a junior at the University of Georgia. At Athens High School, he'd been the captain of both his football and baseball teams, and at the University of Georgia, he was a member of the varsity football and varsity baseball teams. Legendary Georgia football coach Harry Mehre once made the statement that "Ed Hamilton and Tommy Moran are the greatest competitive athletes I have coached."[15]

The university's newspaper recognized Ed as one of several Georgia students who flew regularly at the Athens airport. After a year of study with Ben, Ed was a candidate for a pilot's license.[16] Ed decided to leave the School of Commerce at Georgia in June 1931, before his senior year, and took the Army Air Corps entrance exam at Montgomery, Alabama. He scored the highest mark ever awarded on the aviation school entrance exam at the time and attended the Army Air Corps training school in San Antonio, Texas.[17] While training in Texas, Ed sent Ben a photograph of himself and a photograph of one of the planes he was flying.[18] A year later he was commissioned a second lieutenant and sent to Panama.[19] He continued to exchange letters with Ben.

While serving in Panama, Ed had an opportunity to put into practice the emergency measures that he'd learned from Ben. He was flying at 3,000 feet over dense jungle on 19 September 1932. Suddenly, half of his propeller broke off, resulting in severe vibration that caused the motor to tear out and fall under the plane. The plane instantly went into a steep dive. Ed tried to jump out, but his parachute caught on the cowling. At 800 feet he was finally able to free his parachute. He landed safely in the jungle and was rescued by local residents. After returning to his base, he sent Ben a copy of the newspaper article describing his harrowing ordeal.[20]

The 1930s got off to a great start for Ben: he was settling into a new home, developing a new plane design, setting new aviation records, receiving recognition in a national aviation magazine, and fostering a growing aviation school. Ben didn't know it at the time, but this was the pinnacle of his career. The years ahead would be marred by tragedies and failures. They would be the most difficult years of his life.

John Edward Epps was the first child born to Omie and Ben after their move into the city. He was born on 23 June 1931, their sixth son. Tragically, he didn't live to celebrate his first birthday. Late on Tuesday, 30 May 1932, an automobile struck eleven-month-old John Edward in the front yard of the new home on Hill Street. He died at the hospital in the early morning hours the following day. The comment Ben made to Omie prior to his agreeing to move into the city about the danger the city posed to their children sadly turned out to be prescient. It was any parent's worst nightmare come true, but this particular tragedy was a double heartbreak for Ben and Omie: the automobile that struck John Edward was driven by Ben Jr.[21]

Ben's brother, Roy, died in March 1931, and now, a year later, his youngest son died. The family experienced two grievous deaths in two years, and this string of yearly deaths was not going to end soon.

The following year, on 14 March 1933, twenty-five-year-old Ed Hamilton was killed in the Canal Zone when the pursuit plane he was piloting during maneuvers collided with another plane. The fiery crash was witnessed by hundreds of residents of the Canal Zone who'd turned out to watch the maneuvers.[22]

Ed's body was brought back to Athens and lay in state at First Methodist Church. There was an honorary escort composed of sixty members of the university ROTC cavalry unit; sixty members of the university infantry unit; eighteen staff officers of the Athens High School military unit; a detachment from the local American Legion post; and another from the Athens Officers Reserve Association; along with Dr. S. V. Sanford, president of the university; Thomas W. Reed, registrar; several professors who taught Ed when he was a student at the university; members of the university coaching staff; and Ben Epps. A squadron of twelve planes from Langley Field, Virginia, flew over the church during the services and flew over his grave during the burial ceremony at Oconee Hill Cemetery.[23]

A memorial service for Ed was also held at the military post in the Canal Zone. As part of this service, the Army Air Corps flew an aerial salute known as the "Missing Man Formation" over the large crowd that had gathered to honor Ed. Ben obtained a photograph of this "Missing Man Formation," which he kept in his scrapbook along with a newspaper article from the Canal Zone about Ed's death.[24] The string of annual deaths continued.

In 1934, Ben's friend, Doug Davis, one of America's most famous airplane pilots, won the Bendix Trophy in a cross-country race from Burbank, California, to Cleveland, Ohio. He remained in Cleveland, where a few days later he won the Unlimited Shell Speed Dash, exceeding the world's landplane speed record of 304.98 miles per hour. A few hours after that triumph, he would be competing for the Thompson Trophy at the Cleveland National Air Races, an event he'd won in 1929.[25]

Nearly 100,000 spectators gathered to watch the twelve-lap, 100-mile race, which was the final racing event of that year's program. On the eighth lap, Doug was leading the field by an eighth-mile margin. Flying at 250 miles per hour, he cut inside a pylon. His plane suddenly shot out of control and twisted through the air as it plunged nose-first into the ground. Doug was nearly decapitated and his body was badly mangled. The thirty-three-year-old was survived by a wife, a six-year-old son, and a four-year-old daughter. Ben was able to obtain a photograph of Doug that was taken in Cleveland just before the Thompson Trophy Race. A note written in pen on this photograph reads, "Made at Cleveland Just Before Race. Last Photo of Douglas Davis."[26] Doug was enshrined in the Georgia Aviation Hall of Fame on 18 May 1991.[27]

While Ben was struggling with these deaths of family and friends, another calamity was in the making; it was called the Great Depression. It began with Wall Street's crash on 29 October 1929, when stock prices plummeted. That day would forever be known as "Black Tuesday." The Great Depression reached its lowest point during winter 1933–1934, and it was the longest, most widespread, and deepest economic depression of the twentieth century. Unemployment reached a level of 25 percent, while poverty and the number of homeless soared. This economic apocalypse struck a severe financial blow to Ben's garage business. The possibility of having to close his business because he couldn't pay the rent weighed heavily on him. Also, without paying customers, he couldn't afford to fly his planes. But even worse, he didn't know how he was going to feed and clothe his children.

Omie and Ben had another son on 23 February 1934, Ernest Patrick. He was their first child born since the death of John Edward. They now had eight children to raise, and the growing strain on Ben was staggering.

One of the ways Ben dealt with stress was to exercise. He'd been an active member of the Athens YMCA since 1909, and he always took great pride in staying physically fit. He played basketball, swam, and worked out at the "Y." At forty-seven years of age, Ben was observed at the YMCA "walking about on his hands, keeping perfect balance with no strain of any kind in evidence" and "he looks to be about 30."[28]

But the best way to deal with stress in Ben's view was to do what he loved most—fly his plane. There was a certain peace and serenity in a powder-blue sky, where he could leisurely bank his plane back and forth, soar in sweeping circles, and pass through billowy, white clouds. It was the perfect escape from the crushing pressures on the ground below.[29] But there were no billowy, white clouds in Ben's sky anymore; perilous storm clouds were on the horizon and fast approaching.

Ben had two paying customers at the airfield on Sunday afternoon, 3 March 1935, Sylvia Raskin and Bernard Freeman. Sylvia Raskin, twenty years old, was from Savannah. She'd come to Athens for the weekend to attend the Kappa Alpha masquerade ball and was staying with girlfriends at the Delta Phi Epsilon sorority house.

Bernard Freeman was a sophomore at Georgia from New York City.[30] Raskin and Freeman were interested in a plane ride to see Athens and the surrounding area from the sky. Ben seated his two customers in his 1930 Epps XII Light Biplane with the de Havilland Gipsy engine and took off on the sightseeing outing.

It was approaching 6:00 P.M. when the plane crossed over downtown Athens heading back to the airfield on Lexington Road. Without warning, something went terribly wrong. Ben was suddenly in a desperate fight to keep the nose of the plane up. He succeeded twice, but not a third time. The plane went into a fatal, downward spin.

A witness on the ground, K. O. Franks, coming across the YMCA athletic field, saw the plane make two circles, as if it was performing stunts. The engine popped twice, like an automobile motor backfiring, then quit running. Suddenly, the plane nosed over and spiraled toward the ground. As Franks watched in horror, "the plane came almost straight down."[31]

Another witness, university student John Gordon, heard the plane and looked up just as the engine quit running and the plane started its fatal tailspin. It plunged straight down, 300 feet.[32] The impact was so forceful it shook the ground when it hit in the backyard of a residence on Lumpkin Street, across from the present-day Fine Arts building on the University of Georgia campus.[33]

Sylvia Raskin was killed instantly; she was an only child. Her companion, Bernard Freeman, suffered a broken leg above the right ankle and a broken heel. He was rushed to Athens General Hospital, where doctors thought his leg might have to be amputated. Ben suffered a broken hip and was taken to St. Mary's Hospital.[34] The story of the crash was covered by the *New York Times*.[35]

Witness K. O. Franks recovered Freeman's blood-stained wristwatch at the scene and told a reporter that it had stopped running at 5:51 P.M. University student Gordon helped pull Ben out of the wreckage and said that Ben was still conscious but in shock and didn't say anything.

The *Athens Banner-Herald* commented that Ben lived "a charmed life," as he had escaped with his life from previous serious crashes. But just like his other crashes, in which he "suffered serious injuries, once being confined for weeks to a hospital bed,"[36] his injuries were serious this time, too. Three days later Ben still had "not regained full consciousness."[37] It was not until the end of that week that he showed improvement.[38] He was eventually released from the hospital, but it took months for him to recover.[39]

Not being able to work, Ben could no longer afford to keep his garage open. He'd struggled financially for years and tried every way he could to maintain his garage business, but the debilitating injuries from the crash made that impossible. He was forced to close his garage at 392 East Washington Street, where he'd worked since December 1910.[40] Ben was not physically able to clean out his equipment and personal belongings from the garage. He was thus spared from what would have been an emotionally draining, painful task. Instead, Ben Jr. was sent to clean out and close down Epps Garage.[41]

When it seemed to Ben that things couldn't get any worse, they did. Fewer than three months after the fatal plane crash on Lumpkin Street, Ben was confronted with another loss. His father died at the family residence on West Hancock Avenue on 25 May 1935. Thomas Epps was seventy-seven years old.[42]

Ben finally recovered to the point of being able to work again, but with his garage now closed, he had to find a new job in order to feed his family. After a lengthy search, Ben found employment with the U.S. Department of Interior. He worked for the federal government as an automobile mechanic at the Federal Building Warehouse in Athens.[43] The job only paid thirty-five dollars a week, but it allowed him time and some money to get back into flying.[44] It also allowed him to slowly start rebuilding his business of buying and selling used airplanes.[45]

Still scarred emotionally from the death of the young girl in the 1935 crash and the loss of his father and his garage, Ben immersed himself in a new project—rebuilding his wrecked plane. His goal was to sell the plane and generate some much-needed cash.[46] Ben worked on this rebuilding project in a small, wooden building on the corner of West Washington Street and Pulaski Street. He was helped on occasion by Loyd Florence, a friend of the Epps family.[47]

The advertisement for Ben's rebuilt plane was answered by Harold Cagle. A few years after graduating from Athens High School, Cagle and a friend were considering buying Ben's de Havilland Gipsy biplane. On a Saturday afternoon, 16 October 1937, Ben and Cagle took off in the plane from the Athens airport.

Cagle had flown in the plane before with Ben, but this was the first time Cagle was in the pilot's seat. Ben was instructing him on how to operate the plane's controls. The plane was fifty yards into the air on takeoff, climbing at a steep angle. With no warning, the plane nosed-over and went straight into the ground.[48]

Cagle was taken to the hospital in serious condition with "a badly crushed left ankle, an injured head and minor cuts and bruises about the face and body." It was feared that the injured leg of the former fullback and track athlete "may have to be amputated."[49]

Ben was alive but unconscious when he was pulled from the wreckage. His twelve-year-old son, Charles, was at the airport when the crash occurred and helped to pull his father from the plane. Ben had "a small basil fracture of the skull" and was rushed to Athens General Hospital. He died several hours later, never having regained consciousness.[50]

Omie was distraught. She lamented out loud that she didn't know how she was going to be able to raise her children. The youngest child, Rosemond Claire, had been born on 29 March 1935. Ben was survived by Omie and nine children, ranging in age from two to twenty-two years old. They faced a financial burden even more extreme than they'd already endured.

Omie cried for two straight days and then stopped. She focused on her children, put on the best face possible, and did what she had to do. She lived one day at a time and took every adversity that came her way in stride. She would do whatever it took to care for and raise her children.[51]

After decades of pursuing his passion for planes without reaping any financial benefits, having lost his garage business, and with the country still mired in the Great Depression, Ben was in an impossibly deep financial hole at the time of his death. Without Omie's knowledge, he'd mortgaged the house on Hill Street to stay afloat, something he had told her he would never do. The family was left with only enough money to bury him. "He had lost everything we had," Omie told her interviewer in 1939, in a heart-wrenching portrayal of what her life had been like since Ben's death.[52]

At the time of this interview (1939), Omie was selling cosmetics out of the trunk of her car in order to pay the bills for her and the children. She also sold Christmas cards during the Christmas season. When she made sales calls, she had to take the two youngest children with her and would leave them in the car. These sales calls were where her "few pennies come from now."[53]

Omie's sales calls became so difficult that at one point she talked of taking boarders into her home so she could give up selling her cosmetics and stay at home. But her two oldest boys didn't like the idea of strangers living in the family home.[54] Besides, the house was already overcrowded with the children. A few years earlier the basement was excavated to add another room, which the two oldest boys were using as their bedroom. There was simply no place to put a boarder.[55]

Omie had worked all her life and said she knew what it took to live. Although she struggled to keep her head above water financially, she added, "Some days I do real well, and some days I get so discouraged I feel like giving up, but I can't."[56]

Omie also confided that she was saddened that Ben died feeling like he'd been a failure. But she wouldn't listen to any of that talk. Her husband, who'd been taken away from her at such a young age, had left behind a house full of children that they both could be proud of having raised. She had always been proud of Ben, too, and admired the fact that no matter how bad things seemed, he'd always, somehow, managed to provide his family with what he thought they needed.[57]

Of greater importance than his having been the provider for his family, Ben gave himself to his family. No amount of money or material items could compete with the value of the time he gave them. He knew well that children do not need things, they need parents, and on that level Ben excelled. That quality alone made Ben a resounding success in Omie's eyes...and heart.

Ben's legacy to his children was his character, which he instilled in each of them. He didn't just sit in a church pew on Sunday morning, he took the things he learned in life and put them into practice; he was a doer. One event in particular epitomizes Ben's character.

On the morning of 4 March 1925, Ben and a friend left Athens on a trip to Florida in Ben's car. They drove through Madison, Georgia, and were about eight miles from Eatonton when Ben noticed a man walking unsteadily in a field headed away from the highway. The man's hat was slouched over his face and he appeared to be bleeding. Ben pulled over and went to check on the man. He was bleeding profusely from a hole on top of his head. Ben helped the man back to the car and put him in the front seat, then drove to Eatonton to find medical help.

On the way, the man talked only brokenly as Ben and his friend questioned him as to his name and what had happened. The man said his name was W. C. Wright and that he lived in Eatonton. He spoke incoherently but was able to convey that he'd stopped to pick up two hitchhikers and now had a hole in his head and his car was missing. He could remember little else before passing out. Ben learned later that Wright was the sixty-seven-year-old school superintendent of Putnam County. One of the best known educators in the state of Georgia, and Wright had previously served as president of the Georgia Education Association. The story of the assault and Ben's heroics were headline material in newspapers across the state. Unfortunately, Wright died from his wounds on 7 March.[58]

In addition to his children, Ben taught countless numbers of students to fly and instilled in them, as he did his children, a love of aviation. A long list of names of the pilots whom Ben taught was recorded in the *Athens Banner-Herald*, in a 3 May 1931 article.[59]

Ben had a profound influence on the lives of many people. Perhaps the most endearing tribute Omie received after his death was in a letter dated 17 November 1937. It came from New York City, and the sender had only learned that morning of Ben's death, "a very sad and disappointing shock."[60] The letter lauded Ben as an individual who

> did much to enhance [aviation's] future and progress in Georgia. He was unfortunate in having limited material and extremely bad breaks against him. No one can ever condemn him for his misfortunes and I am sure that God understands he had a useful life and did his best to make this humdrum world a more exciting place to live in.
>
> My family and I extend our deepest sympathies and may God bless you all.[61]

The author of this letter was Bernard F. Freeman, the same Bernard F. Freeman who had been involved in Ben's 3 March 1935 plane crash that killed Sylvia Raskin.

Of great significance to all Georgians, Ben left behind an incredible legacy as the state's first aviator and the first person in the United States to fly a monoplane. Omie would add that she was sure

Ben would have been happy to know that he had "died [doing]...what he loved best."[62]

As Omie recalled the events in her life, she reflected,

> You know, a mother of ten children and nine living don't [sic] have time to think about what has happened, and I'm afraid to think what might take [sic] place, after all I have been through. I have had children, and my husband has been killed.
>
> I am praying I won't have to go through it again. We never know what is to happen to us in this life.[63]

Omie continued to live in the house at 892 Hill Street and raise her children. Loyd Florence, a friend of the Epps family, described her as "always smiling...she was just a happy person, and I think that a lot of the credit to the success of the Epps's children is really due to Mrs. Epps."[64] She lived in the Hill Street residence until her death, dying in her sleep at the house on 19 June 1965. Omie was seventy-one years old and survived by her nine children and twenty-five grandchildren. She did not have to endure the death of a child or husband again. Omie is buried next to Ben in Oconee Hill Cemetery, Athens, Georgia.[65]

EPILOGUE

On 28 August 1909, two remarkable men, twenty-one-year-old Ben Epps and nineteen-year-old Zumpt Huff, made national history in Athens, Georgia. They built a monoplane that was the first monoplane to fly in the United States and the first plane of any type to fly in the state of Georgia. It was an achievement that not even the Wright brothers had accomplished. Their story epitomizes the American spirit and is one of the strands of fabric in the historical tapestry of American exceptionalism. To paraphrase a line from a character in George Bernard Shaw's play *Back to Methuselah*, Ben and Zumpt dared to dream the unimaginable and asked, "Why not?"[1]

With only a dream, Ben and Zumpt set out against seemingly insurmountable odds to achieve the impossible. Fueled by a tireless passion and spirited optimism, they persevered through numerous failed attempts. They never feared failure because they knew failure was a great teacher that could provide valuable feedback. It was the mechanism that taught them how to succeed.

Ben and Zumpt's journey to build a heavier-than-air machine capable of flight had them cross paths with some of the most world-renowned icons of the time. Ultimately, Ben Epps and Zumpt Huff opened the door that brought the age of air travel to Georgia, the state that would one day lay claim to the home of the nation's busiest airport, both in passengers and number of flights, Atlanta's Hartsfield-Jackson International Airport.[2]

Neither man sought fame or celebrity status for what he accomplished, and neither man obsessed about the pursuit of wealth. Both were quiet, hardworking men who believed family came first. The children they raised and the many descendants that have followed are testimony to the achievement Ben and Zumpt thought most important.[3]

History should have been kinder to these men while they were alive and given them the recognition their many achievements deserved. But that is often the case when it comes to pioneers. Fully understanding the significance of the accomplishment sometimes comes years, or even decades, later.

For Benjamin Thomas Epps, Sr., the past fifty years have seen his accomplishments acknowledged, to an extent. There have been many articles about his contribution to aviation, the airport in Athens bears his name, he was inducted into the Georgia Aviation Hall of Fame, and an annual aerospace innovation award for the state of Georgia is named in his honor. But this recognition will not be complete until the National Aviation Hall of Fame in Dayton, Ohio, officially recognizes the Epps-Huff partnership's 1909 Epps-Huff III Monoplane as the first monoplane to fly in the United States.

Zumpt Alston Huff, on the other hand, once lauded as part of a team that was Georgia's version of the Wright brothers, was forgotten after he left Athens at the end of 1910. He, too, should be recognized by the National Aviation Hall of Fame and deserves a place in the Georgia Aviation Hall of Fame next to his former partner. You cannot put one "Wright brother" in the Hall of Fame and leave the other one out.

After more than one hundred years, it can now be said that the account of the first flight of a monoplane in the United States and the first airplane flight of any kind in the state of Georgia has been told. The story will be preserved for the ages and serve as an inspiration to future generations. The men behind the Epps-Huff partnership would be proud.

Appendix

Chronology of Plane Designs

<u>Epps-Huff Partnership Plane Designs</u>:
Designs Inspired by 1903 Wright Flyer:

Epps-Huff I – Biplane	May 1909
Epps-Huff II - Monoplane	June/July 1909
Epps-Huff III – Monoplane	August 1909 – First plane to fly
Epps-Huff IV – Monoplane	December 1909

Designs Inspired by Blériot XI:

Epps-Huff V – Monoplane	Spring 1910
Epps-Huff VI – Monoplane	Fall 1910

<u>Ben T. Epps, Sr. Post-Partnership Plane Designs</u>:

Epps VII – Monoplane	February 1911
Epps VIII – Monoplane	1912 – First plane with ailerons
Epps IX – Monoplane	1914-1915
Epps X – Biplane	Spring 1916
Epps XI – Light Monoplane	Summer 1924
Epps XII – Light Biplane	June 1930 – "Rockeagle"

Bibliography

Manuscript Collections
Benjamin Thomas Epps Papers, Hargrett Rare Book and Manuscript Library, University of Georgia Libraries: Athens.

Books and Articles
Allen, Frederick. *Atlanta Rising: The Invention of an International City 1946–1996*. Atlanta: Longstreet Press, 1996.

Banham, Russ. *The Ford Country: Ford Motor Company and the Innovations That Shaped the World*. New York: Artisan, 2002.

Bryan, Ford Richardson. *Beyond the Model T: The Other Ventures of Henry Ford*. Detriot: Wayne State University Press, 1997.

Crouch, Tom D. *The Bishop's Boys: A Life of Wilbur and Orville Wright*. New York: W. W. Norton & Co, 2003.

"Eminent Georgians." *Southern Society of Research & History*. Vol. 1. Edited by Robert Paul Turbeville. Decatur, GA: Browne Press, 1937.

Galt, Evelyn Epps, "Epps, Benjamin Thomas" in *Dictionary of Georgia Biography*. Vol. 1. Edited by Kenneth Coleman and Charles Stephen Gurr. Athens: University of Georgia Press, 1983.

Garrett, Franklin M. (1954) 1969. *Atlanta and Environs*. Vol. 2. Reprint, Athens: University of Georgia Press.

Gibbons, Edward. *Floyd Gibbons—Your Headline Hunter*. New York: Exposition Press, 1953.

Gray, Edith Stearns. *UP: A True Story of Aviation*. Strasburg, VA: Shenandoah Publishing House, 1931.

Homan, Andrew. *Life in the Slipstream: The Legend of Bobby Walthour, Sr.* Dulles, VA: Potomac Books, 2001.

Hornsby, Sadie B., "An Air-Minded Family," in *Athens Memories: The WPA Federal Writers' Project Interviews*. Edited by Al Hester. Athens, GA: Green Berry Press, 2001.

Keen, Jennifer D. *World War I*. Westport, CT: Greenwood Press, 2006.

Lewis, David L. *The Public Image of Henry Ford an American Folk Hero and His Company*. Detroit: Wayne State University Press, 1987.

Milton, Edwin. *A History of Hapeville*. Alpharetta, GA: W. H. Wolfe Associates, 1991.

Our Family Tree, Ficquett-Wilbanks-Huff, Extended Families, 1788-1995. Edited by Thora O. Kimsey. Monroe, GA: T. O. Kimsey, 1995.

Pattillo, Donald M. *A History in the Making: 80 Turbulent Years in the American General Aviation Industry.* New York: McGraw-Hill, 1998.

Reese, Gussie. *This They Remembered, 1851–1865.* Washington, GA: Washington Publishing, 1965.

Rowe, Hugh. (1923) 2000. *History of Athens and Clarke County.* Reprint, Greenville, SC: Southern Historical Press, 2000.

Shaw, George Bernard. *Back to Methuselah (A Metabiological Pentateuch).* New York: Brentano's, 1921.

Stoff, Joshua. *Images of America, Long Island Aircraft Crashes, 1909–1959.* New York: Arcadia Publishing, 2004.

Tate, Susan B., "Reed, Thomas W," in *Dictionary of Georgia Biography.* Vol. 2. Edited by Kenneth Coleman and Charles Stephen Gurr. Athens: University of Georgia Press, 1983.

Thomas, Frances Taliaferro. *A Portrait of Historic Athens and Clarke County.* Athens: University of Georgia Press, 1992.

Who's Who in the South, 1927. Washington, DC: Mayflower Publishing Co., 1927.

Zarnowitz, Victor. *Business Cycles: Theory, History, Indicators and Forecasting.* Chicago: University of Chicago Press, 1996.

Newspapers and Periodicals

Aerial Age Weekly
Air & Space Smithsonian Magazine
Athens (GA) *Banner*
Athens (GA) *Banner-Herald*
Athens (GA) *Banner-Herald & Daily News*
Athens (GA) *Daily Banner*
Athens (GA) *Daily Herald*
Athens (GA) *Magazine*
Athens (GA) *Weekly Banner*
Atlanta Constitution
Atlanta Constitution Magazine
Atlanta Georgian & News
Atlanta Journal
Atlanta Journal & Constitution
Atlanta Journal Magazine
Augusta (GA) *Chronicle*
Banner-Watchman (Athens, GA)

Charlotte (NC) *Observer*
Dublin (GA) *Courier-Herald*
Eatonton (GA) *Messenger*
Florida Times-Union (Jacksonville, FL)
Grand Rapids (MI) *Press*
Lenoir (NC) *News-Topic*
Macon (GA) *News*
New York Times
North-East Georgia (Athens, GA)
Oglethorpe Echo (Lexington, GA)
Popular Aviation
Popular Mechanics
Red and Black (Athens, GA)
Savannah (GA) *Morning News*
Science
Southern Banner (Athens, GA)
Southern Watchman (Athens, GA)
Sport Aviation
Valdosta (GA) *Times*
Washington (DC) *Post*
Weekly Banner-Watchman (Athens, GA)
Winder (GA) *News*

Films
Ben Epps, The Legacy of Georgia's First Aviator. DVD. Written and produced by William J. Evelyn. Athens: University of Georgia, 2001.

Public Records
Clarke County, Georgia Records, Clerk of Superior Court's Office, Athens, GA
Clarke County, Georgia Records, Clerk of Probate Court's Office, Athens, GA
Franklin County, Georgia Records, Clerk of Superior Court's Office Carnesville, GA
Franklin County, Georgia Records, Clerk of Probate Court's Office Carnesville, GA
Madison County, Georgia Records, Clerk of Superior Court's Office Danielsville, GA
Madison County, Georgia Records, Clerk of Probate Court's Office Danielsville, GA

Twelfth Census of the United States (1900)

Websites

Aerodacious, accessed 1 August 2015,
  http://www.aerodacious.com/ccAM098.htm.

Aerofiles, Capsule Biographies, accessed 3 August 2015,
  http://www.aeroflies.com/bio_w.html.

Aerospace, accessed 4 August 2015,
  http://www.aerospaceweb.org/question/history/q0103.shtml.

Athens Banner-Herald, "Statue honoring Georgia's first pilot installed at
  Athens City Hall," 26 November 2015, accessed 15 July 2013,
  http://onlineathens.com.

Bicycle Club of Atlanta, accessed 4 August 2015,
  http://www.oldbike.com/Walthour.html.

Biography Base, accessed 1 August 2015,
  http://www.biographybase.com/biography/Bleriot_Louis.html.

British Anzani Company History Page, accessed 4 August 2015,
  http://www.britishanzani.co.uk/AnzHist.htm.

Daniels, Mark, "Anzani," accessed 24 February 2009,
  http://www.icenicam.ukfsn.org/-articles1/art0019.html.

Early Aviators, accessed 3 August 2015,
  http://www.earlyaviators.com/ehistory.htm.

E–M–F History Page, accessed 4 August 2015,
  http://www.emfauto.org/EMF_history.php.

Epps Aviation, accessed 6 August 2015, www.eppsaviation.com/about/.

Epps, Benjamin Thomas, Scrapbook, accessed 5 August 2015,
  http://www.fax.libs.uga.edu/Ms3074/p/iMs3074p.html.

Epps Family Cousins Club, accessed 5 August 2015,
  http://www.reocities.com/Heartland/oaks/4050/epps.htm.

Georgia Aviation Hall of Fame, accessed 1 August 2015,
  http://www.gaaviationhalloffame.com/Hall-of-
  Fame.48.0.html?avid=35.

Georgia Digital Newspapers, accessed 8 August 2015,
  http://dig.gallileo.usg.edu/MediaTypes/Newspapers.

Glenn H. Curtiss Museum, accessed 4 August 2015,
  http://www.glennhcurtissmuseum.org/educational/glenn_curtiss.html.

Hartsfield-Jackson Atlanta International Airport, accessed 1 August 2015,
  http://www.atlanta-airport.com/Airport/ATL/ATL_FactSheet.aspx.

History of Air Racing and Record-Breaking Pilots, accessed 5 August 2015,
  http://www.air-racing-history.com/PILOTS/Doug%20Davis.htm.

Library of Congress, American Life Histories: Manuscripts from the Federal
    Writers' Project, 1936–1940, accessed 4 August 2015,
    http:///www.loc.gov/item/wpalh000513/.
Military Factory, accessed 4 August 2015,
    http://www.militaryfactory.com/aircraft/detail.asp?aircraft_id=713.
Monash College, "The Pioneers," accessed 1 August 2015,
    http://www.ctiemonash.edu.au/hargrave/beleriot.html.
Museum of Flight, accessed 5 August 2015,
    http://www.museumofflight.org/aircraft/alexander-eaglerock.
National Aeronautics and Space Administration, Glenn Research Center,
    accessed 4 August 2015, http://www.grc.nasa.gov/WWW/k-
    12/airplane/air.html.
National Aeronautics and Space Administration, U.S. Centennial of Flight
    Commission, accessed 19 September 2012,
    http://www.centennialofflight.gov.essay/Dictionary/Bleriot/DI11html.
National Aviation Hall of Fame, accessed 3 August 2015,
    http://www.nationalaviation.org/walden-henry/.
Online Etymology Dictionary, accessed 4 August 2015,
    http://www.etymonline.com/index.php?search=aileron.
Peachstate Aerodrome, "Candler Field Museum History," accessed 1 August
    2015, http://www.peachstateaero.com/museum/.
Radio Days, accessed 7 August 2015, www.otr.com/gibbons.shtml.
Weider History Group, "Bill Piper and the Piper Cubs," accessed 5 August
    2015, http://www.historynet.com/bill-piper-and-the-piper-cubs.htm.
World Airport Codes, accessed 1 August 2015, http://www.world-airport-
    codes.com/world-top-30-airports.html.
World War I, www.worldwar1.com/sffgbw.htm.
Wright Airplane Co., www.first-to-
    fly.com/History/Wright%20Story/heflies.htm.
Wright Brothers History. First Airplane Flight, http://ww.wright-in-
    house.com/wright-brothers/.

Historical Markers
Georgia Historical Marker, No. 029-16 (Athens-Clarke County-Ben Epps
    Airport/Erected 1987)
Georgia Historical Marker, No. 29-5 (120 East Washington Street/Erected
    2007)
Georgia Historical Marker, No. 108-1 (Oconee County Courthouse/Erected
    1954)

Exhibits
Georgia Aviation Hall of Fame, Museum of Aviation, Warner Robbins Air
force Base, Warner Robbins, GA

Directories
Athens City Directory, 1904, 1909, 1920–1921, 1931, 1937
Atlanta City Directory, 1908, 1909, 1910, 1911, 1912, 1913, 1914, 1915,
1916, 1925, 1926

Author Interviews
Benson, Thomas J.
Epps, Patrick
Gensheimer, Teresa Laughlin
Halyard, Mary Jane Huff
Halyard, Paul

Notes

Prologue

[1] "Aviator, 2 companies honored at Epps gala," *Athens* (GA) *Banner-Herald*, 23 October 2007, A7; "Anniversary Events," *Athens Magazine* 19/1 (March/April 2007). The Ben T. Epps Aerospace Innovation Awards recognize outstanding achievement in three categories: aviation educator, aviator innovator, and aviation invention. Governor Sonny Purdue was originally scheduled to present the awards at the gala but was unable to attend.

[2] "100 years of flight, Celebrating the Epps Legacy," *Athens Magazine* 19/1 (March/April 2007): cover.

[3] Georgia Historical Marker No. 029-16, "Georgia's Pioneer Aviator, Ben T. Epps, 1888–1937," at Athens-Clarke County-Ben Epps Airport, Athens-Clarke County, Georgia/Erected in 1987.

[4] "Epps, Ben T." Georgia Aviation Hall of Fame, Century of Flight Hangar, Museum of Aviation, Robbins Air Force Base, Warner Robbins, Georgia, plaque; accessed 1 August 2015, http://www.gaaviationhalloffame.com/Hall-of-Fame.48.0.html?avid=35.

[5] Blake Aued, "Statue honoring Georgia's first pilot installed at Athens City Hall," *OnlineAthens, Athens* (GA) *Banner-Herald*, 26 November 2011; accessed 15 July 2013, http://www.onlineathens.com.

[6] Pate McMichael, "A Wing and a Prayer," *Athens Magazine* 19/1 (March/April 2007): 20.

[7] *Who's Who in the South, 1927*, s.v. Hugh J. Rowe (Washington, DC: Mayflower Publishing Co., 1927) 630; Southern Society of Research and History, *Eminent Georgians*, vol.1, ed. Robert Paul Turbeville, s.v. "Hugh J. Rowe" (Decatur, GA: Browne Press, 1937).

[8] Hugh J. Rowe, "Did It Ever Occur to 'U'," *Athens* (GA) *Banner-Herald*, 22 January 1939, 4A.

[9] Thomas W. Reed, "Echoes from Memoryland," *Athens* (GA) *Banner-Herald*, 3 September 1947, 4. In this first column Reed wrote, "Sixty-two years have rolled by since I came to Athens as a fifteen year old college boy....

These contributions will not all be reminiscent in their nature. Some of them may be pure fiction...some may be the recounting of historic happenings." See also, "Biographical Files," The Georgia Room, Richard Russell Library, University of Georgia Libraries, Athens, s.v. "Thomas W. Reed." Reed was born in Atlanta on 20 September 1870. In addition to an undergraduate degree from the University of Georgia, Reed also earned a law degree at UGA. See also Susan B. Tate, "Reed, Thomas W.," in *Dictionary of Georgia Biography*, vol. 2, eds. Kenneth Coleman and Charles Stephen Gurr (Athens: University of Georgia Press, 1983) 829.

[10] Thomas W. Reed, "Echoes from Memoryland: The Late Ben Epps and the Flying Machine He Built," *Athens* (GA) *Banner-Herald*, 1 March 1949, 4. There are seemingly irreconcilable differences between Rowe's and Reed's accounts of the first flight. Reed's article says the first flight was at night and only mentions a few witnesses being present to watch. Rowe's article does not mention the flight occurring at night and says that a "large crowd" was present. The reason for these discrepancies is explained in chapter 6.

[11] Tom Dunkin, "Ben Epps—Georgia's Pioneer in the Sky," *Atlanta Journal & Constitution*, 31 July 1966, 1-C. At least one subsequent article uses Todd's precise description of the flight, without citing Todd as the source, to describe the first flight. See Dean Looney, "Athens aviator Ben Epps's impact still a lofty one," *Athens* (GA) *Banner-Herald*, 31 October 1987, 1.

[12] "Blériot, Louis," biographybase, accessed 1 August 2015, http://www.biographybase.com/biography/Bleriot_Louis.html; "Blériot, Louis," National Aeronautics and Space Administration, U.S. Centennial of Flight Commission, accessed 19 September 2012, http://www.centennialofflight.gov.essay/Dictionary/Bleriot/DI11html.

[13] Rowe, "Did It Ever Occur to 'U'," 4A.

[14] Lola Trammell, "Man Who Put Georgia in the Air," *Atlanta Journal Magazine*, 27 March 1949, 8.

[15] "Flatwoods," *Oglethorpe Echo* (Lexington, GA), 5 November 1909, 10. See also "Street Corner Gossip," *Athens* (GA) *Banner*, 12 November 1909, 8.

[16] "Flying Machine Near Lexington," *Oglethorpe Echo* (Lexington, GA), 3 September 1909, 5.

Chapter 1

[1] Evelyn Epps Galt, "Epps, Benjamin Thomas," in *Dictionary of Georgia Biography*, vol. 1, eds. Kenneth Coleman and Charles Stephen Gurr (Athens: University of Georgia Press, 1983) 293.

[2] Georgia Historical Marker No. 108-1, "Oconee County, Georgia," at Oconee County Courthouse, Watkinsville, Georgia/Erected 1954. Oconee County was created by an act of the state legislature on 25 February 1875, with Watkinsville as the county seat. Watkinsville was the county seat of Clarke County when the county was founded in 1801 and remained so until 1871, when it was replaced by Athens.

[3] Galt, "Epps," *Georgia Biography*, 293.

[4] Epps Family Cousins Club, accessed 5 August 2015: http://reocities.com/Heartland/oaks/4050/epps.htm.

[5] Warranty Deed dated 1890 listing the grantee as "Thomas J. Epps of Oconee County." Clarke County, Clerk of Superior Court's Office, Athens, Georgia, Deed Book HH, page 281.

[6] "Georgia, Clark [*sic*], County, to the Ordinary of said County," *Banner-Watchman* (Athens, GA), 24 February 1891, 2 (Legal Advertisement).

[7] Galt, "Epps," *Georgia Biography*, 293.

[8] "Election Notice," *Southern Watchman* (Athens, GA), 28 December 1870, 1.

[9] "Analysis of the Public School Law," *Southern Watchman* (Athens, GA), 4 January 1871, 2. This article is a reprint of the analysis of the school law from the *Augusta Constitutionalist.*

[10] "Common Schools," *Southern Watchman* (Athens, GA), 11 February 1874, 2. According to the annual report of State School Superintendent G. J. Orr, for the year ending 1873, there were 198,516 white school-age children in the state and 150,198 black school-age children. Out of these totals only 29.5 percent of white children and 13.3 percent of black students were enrolled in public schools. A very small number of pupils were enrolled in private schools. "School-age children" was defined as children who were six to eighteen years of age.

[11] "The School Election," *Southern Banner* (Athens, GA), 6 January 1871, 3.

[12] A particularly low attendance rate was recorded in 1909 when only 38 percent of the eligible school children in Clarke County attended the public schools. "Grand Jury Presentments," *Athens* (GA) *Banner*, 19 April

1910, 6. (Annual report of the school commissioner, Thomas H. Dozier, to the grand jury, April 1910 term).

[13] "Grand Jury Presentments," *Banner-Watchman* (Athens, GA), 29 May 1883, 3. This grand jury concluded, "The present system of public schools [is] inefficient and as productive of immeasurable injury to the great cause of public education." "Grand Jury Presentments," *Banner-Watchman* (Athens, GA), 27 May 1884, 3. This grand jury believed "that the money expended in the cause [was] at best wasted."

[14] T. L. Gantt, "Public Schools," *Banner-Watchman* (Athens, GA), 1 November 1885, 2. In December 1885, the members of Athens's first board of education were sworn in. See T. L. Gantt, "The Board of Education," *Banner-Watchman* (Athens, GA), 8 December 1885, 2.

[15] "The Board of Education Will Open Public Schools Sept. 1st," *Weekly Banner-Watchman* (Athens, GA), 13 April 1886, 1. This article also notes that Professor E. C. Branson, the first superintendent of the Athens public school system, would arrive in Athens from Washington City the middle of May 1886.

[16] Under this system first through third grade was "primary" school, fourth through sixth grade was "grammar" school, and seventh through ninth "high" school. Tenth grade was not added until 1905.

[17] The white schools were Washington Street, Meigs Street, Oconee Street, and Baxter Street. The black schools were East Athens and West Athens. "Schools Close," *Athens* (GA) *Weekly Banner*, 5 June 1894, 3. The State Negro College of Georgia used the Baxter Street School in summer and fall 1891 for classrooms and lecture halls. In January 1892, Baxter Street School was converted into a white school. "The State Negro College of Georgia Comes Here," *Athens* (GA) *Banner*, 7 November 1891, 1; "The City Schools," *Athens* (GA) *Weekly Banner*, 6 December 1892, 14.

[18] There are no statistics available describing the state of the Clarke County school system in 1894, but there is a published annual report from the school commissioner for the following year. In 1895 the county system operated nineteen schools for white children, with twenty-one white teachers, and twenty-nine schools for black children, with twenty-nine black teachers. None of the schoolhouses was owned by the county board of education. "Grand Jury Presents, April Term 1896," *Athens* (GA) *Weekly Banner*, 8 May 1896, 1. Report of H. R. Bernard, county school commissioner, to the grand jury, dated 1 April 1896. The school budget for 1895 was $3,943. From these funds teachers were paid $3,546, the school

commissioner $300, and $96 was spent on incidentals. The average monthly cost per pupil was $0.89, of which $0.83 was paid by the state.

[19] Ibid. When additional funds became available to the school board in 1902, the school term was increased from five months to six months. See "Grand Jury Presentments," *Athens* (GA) *Weekly Banner*, 25 April 1902, 5. It was not until 1903 that the county schools inaugurated a nine-month term. Clarke County's nine-month session was the first nine-month school system to be established in rural districts of any county in the state with the exception of a few counties where the city and county systems were combined. See "The Rural Schools Are Thriving Under the 9 Months System," *Athens* (GA) *Weekly Banner*, 20 February 1903, 4.

[20] "Grand Jury Presents, April Term 1896," 1. The selection of specific sites for schoolhouses was to be left to the discretion of the board of education and county school commissioner.

[21] "Grand Jury Presentments, October Term 1896," *Athens* (GA) *Weekly Banner*, 6 November 1896, 1. The four schoolhouses and lots were reported as: Winterville, valued at $1,568; Sandy Creek, valued at $304; Princeton, valued at $250; and Chestnut Grove, valued at $200. This grand jury also voted to recommend an additional appropriation of $750 to continue the work of building and improving schoolhouses.

[22] "Public School Building," *Weekly Banner-Watchman* (Athens, GA), 27 April 1886, 1. The Washington Street School was initially called the Market Street School, but when the street it fronted changed names from Market Street to Washington Street in 1888, the name of the school changed. A sketch of the Washington Street School can be viewed in "Our Schools," *Athens* (GA) *Weekly Banner*, 22 April 1890, 5. Ground was broken for the construction of this building in August 1886 (see "Dirt Broken," *Weekly Banner-Watchman* (Athens, GA), 24 August 1886, 1). The school was built on the hill at the rear of the North-Eastern railroad depot, near the center of the old cemetery on Jackson Street. The cemetery at one time extended down and across Broad Street. This location had also served as an Indian burial ground prior to the arrival of white settlers in the area. The newspaper described it at the time as an area where "the dust of two races of people now mingles in the same soil." There were no tombstones, but workmen found some fifteen to twenty unmarked graves when excavation of the foundation was started. The human bones that were unearthed were "gathered together and thrown into a sunken grave nearby, and when the work is finished they will be covered in one common mound.... The graves

are so old that all signs of a coffin have disappeared, and only a few decaying bones and black earth tell where the dead once slept." See "Ghoulish Work," *Banner-Watchman* (Athens, GA), 15 August 1886, 1.

[23] "Prosperous Year in the Public Schools," *Athens* (GA) *Weekly Banner*, 13 July 1900, 8.

[24] "Public Schools of Athens, the Magnificent Record of the Past Eleven Years," *Athens* (GA) *Daily Banner*, 10 December 1897, 16. Earlier the city schools were praised as "peerless among all others in cities the size of Athens." See "Our Schools," 5.

[25] "Prosperous Year," 8. Attendance was worse at the black schools, where only 42 percent of the black school population attended.

[26] Washington Street School did not have a tenth grade class until the Athens City school system offered one in fall 1905. "New Rules Provided for the City Schools," *Athens* (GA) *Banner*, 27 May 1905, 1.

[27] "Closing of City Schools," *Athens* (GA) *Weekly Banner*, 29 May 1903, 7.

[28] Since 1949 the Georgia School of Technology has been officially designated as the Georgia Institute of Technology. Franklin M. Garrett, *Atlanta and Environs*, vol. 2 (1954; repr., Athens: University of Georgia Press, 1969) 173.

[29] Benjamin Thomas Epps Papers, Hargrett Rare Book and Manuscript Library, University of Georgia Libraries, Athens, Georgia 30602 (hereafter cited as "Epps Papers, Hargrett Library"), Box 2, Scrapbook, letter dated 6 November 1903. The contents of Ben Epps's scrapbook can be viewed digitally at "The Benjamin Thomas Epps Scrapbook," accessed 5 August 2015, http://fax.libs.uga.edu/Ms3074/Ms3074p/iMs3074p.html. Ben Epps's 6 November 1903 letter to his parents can be found on this website, pages 9–11 (hereafter references to page numbers of Ben Epps's scrapbook in this collection will be references to the page number where the referenced documents or photographs are found in the digital display at this website). The letter cited above contains a postscript from Ben that he had just received a letter from his parents with $15 enclosed for his November board. He signs the letter, "Your Son, Benjamin T. Epps."

[30] Ibid., 5–6. Letter dated 13 December 1904 from Ben Epps to his parents. The letterhead on the paper had blue letters "G," "T," and "S" superimposed over each other, which stood for "Georgia Technology School."

[31] Mary Jane Halyard, interview with author, 24 January 2009. Mrs. Halyard is a granddaughter of Zumpt and the daughter of Katherine Huff Dulin, Zumpt's oldest child.

[32] *Our Family Tree, Ficquett-Wilbanks-Huff, Extended Families, 1788–1995*, ed. Thora O. Kimsey (Monroe, GA: Thora O. Kimsey, 1995) 178. Zumpt's grandfather, John Peter Huff, was a blacksmith. He enlisted as a private in the 38th Regiment, Georgia Volunteers, Company E, Tom Cobb Infantry (Oglethorpe County) of the Confederate Army. After enlisting in Decatur, Georgia, in April 1862, his company was sent to Savannah and in May 1862 was assigned to General Robert E. Lee's Army of Northern Virginia. He was killed just weeks later on 27 June 1862. Huff was one of seven of his company killed that day and buried the following day on the field of battle "without coffin or shroud." He was forty-seven years old at his death and left behind a forty-year-old widow and eight children. See Gussie Reese, *This They Remembered, 1861–1865* (Washington, GA: Washington Publishing Co., 1965).

[33] Application for Soldier's Pension under Act of 1910, filed by William H. Wilbanks in Franklin County, Clerk of Probate Court's Office, Carnesville, Georgia, No. 3583, Affidavit dated 21 October 1915.

[34] Madison County Marriage Records, Clerk of Probate Court's Office, Danielsville, Georgia, Book C, Page 231.

[35] *Our Family Tree*, 156–57.

[36] Twelfth Census of the United States, Enumeration District No. 28, Sheet No. 20, Franklin County, Georgia, Carnesville 264th District GM, Page 244 A. Enumerated on 25 June 1900. Zumpt's father is also listed as being able to read and write.

[37] *Our Family Tree*, 156–57.

[38] Ibid., 157.

[39] "Building Company Needed," *Athens* (GA) *Weekly Banner*, 7 September 1906, 4. The population of Athens according to the U.S. Census for 1900 was 10,245, and according to a 1904 census of the city it was 13,163.

[40] Advertisement: "Huff's Balm of Gilead," *Oglethorpe Echo* (Lexington, GA), 18 November 1910, 3; Advertisement with a photograph of J. A. Huff: "Huff's Balm of Gilead," *Athens* (GA) *Daily Herald*, 7 September 1916, 8. See also *Our Family Tree*, 168, for a copy of a label from a bottle of James Huff's tonic and physicians' testimonials endorsing the medication.

[41] *Athens* (GA) *City Directory*, 1909.

[42] *Athens* (GA) *City Directory*, 1904 (f).

[43] "Morton & Taylor the New Firm, Electrical Contractors Open Up Business On College Avenue," *Athens* (GA) *Banner*, 11 January 1905, 3.

[44] Advertisements for Morton & Taylor, *Athens* (GA) *Banner*, 21 February 1905, 3; 12 November 1905, 9; 29 November 1905, 2; 30 December 1905, 2.

[45] Advertisement for Morton & Taylor, *Athens* (GA) *Banner*, 12 November 1905, 9.

Chapter 2
[1] Myrtle Huff married Everett P. Taylor on 5 March 1911, in Athens, Georgia. Unfortunately, the marriage did not last. They were divorced in Clarke County Superior Court on 5 April 1926. "Divorce Cases Are Disposed of by Court," *Athens* (GA) *Banner-Herald*, 6 April 1926, 5. "Several divorce cases were disposed of in superior court Monday.... Mrs. Myrtle Huff Taylor versus Everett P. Taylor." Ibid.

[2] There were eighty-four Morton & Taylor Electrical newspaper advertisements in 1905 and sixty-five advertisements in 1906. The last advertisement ran in the *Athens* (GA) *Banner*, 30 August 1906, 2. Morton & Taylor Electrical is last mentioned in the paper as a defendant in a lawsuit that was pending in the Athens City Court, but there is no indication that this civil action had anything to do with the dissolution of this company. See "City Court Docket for Fall Term Completed Yesterday," *Athens* (GA) *Banner*, 2 November 1906, 1. One of the cases on the docket is James Clark, Jr., & Co. vs. Morton & Taylor.

[3] "Personal and Social," *Athens* (GA) *Banner*, 5 February 1908, 2. Joseph Morton married Mamie Jones, daughter of Judge James B. Jones of Toccoa, Georgia.

[4] "E. P. Taylor, Everything Electrical," *Athens* (GA) *Banner*, 2 June 1908, 2. Advertisement. Thirty-nine advertisements were run in the paper for this business in 1908. By 1910 the business was referred to as E. P. Taylor Electrical Contracting and Engineering. Advertisement, "E. P. Taylor Electrical Contracting and Engineering," *Athens* (GA) *Banner*, 1 January 1910, 6.

[5] *Athens* (GA) *City Directory*, 1909.

[6] Evelyn Epps Galt, "Epps, Benjamin Thomas," in *Dictionary of Georgia Biography*, vol. 1, eds. Kenneth Coleman and Charles Stephen Gurr (Athens: University of Georgia Press, 1983) 293.

[7] Advertisement for W. H. Bishop, Motor Cars and Supplies, 120 Washington Street, *Athens* (GA) *Banner*, 28 February 1908, 14. Advertisement for W. H. Bishop, Motor Cars and Supplies, 120 Washington Street, *Athens* (GA) *Banner*, 27 March 1908, 2.

[8] "For Sale: 2 12 g[age] 2nd hand Winchester shot guns. H. B. Sparks, 120 Washington Street," *Athens* (GA) *Banner*, 15 November 1908, 11. See also *Athens* (GA) *Banner*, 12 November 1908, 8 (same advertisement). H. B. Sparks advertisement to sell one two-cylinder Ford automobile at 120 Washington Street, *Athens* (GA) *Banner*, 13 November 1908, 8.

[9] "For Sale: Ford runabout and Cadillac touring car, just overhauled and in good running order. A bargain. Bishop Motor Car Co., Clayton St." *Athens* (GA) *Banner*, 14 March 1909, 7.

[10] *Athens* (GA) *City Directory*, 1909. Walter H. Bishop, located at 133 W. Clayton Street, is listed in this directory under the headings "Automobile Repairing" and "Garage—Automobile." This directory also lists H. B. Sparks' employment as "mechanical engineer" and his employer as "W. H. Bishop Garage."

[11] Ibid.

[12] Warranty Deed to Thomas J. Epps, dated 24 January 1901, for 160 acres on the Middle Oconee River, Clarke County, Georgia, Deed Book 20, page 102. Warranty Deed to Thomas J. Epps, dated 12 December 1903, for 178 acres on Middle Oconee River, near Epps Bridge, Clarke County, Georgia, Deed Book 20, page 164. Warranty Deed to T. J. Epps, dated 22 October 1904, for 18.5 acres on the Middle Oconee River, being part of the old Jennings Mill, a gristmill, Clarke County, Clerk of Superior Court's Office, Athens, Georgia, Deed Book YY, page 205.

[13] T. J. Epps is listed as a resident of Clarke County on the county register of voters in 1902 but does not appear on this register in 1906. See "The Registry List of Rural Districts," *Athens* (GA) *Daily Banner*, 13 May 1902, 3. T. J. Epps is listed as a registered voter in Clarke County's 1467th District–Princeton; "List of Registered Voters of the City of Athens, November 20, 1905," *Athens* (GA) *Banner*, 21 November 1905, 5. (No listing for T. J. Epps); "Sixty Four New Names on Registration List," *Athens* (GA) *Weekly Banner*, 17 August 1906, 5. (No listing for T. J. Epps). T. J. Epps purchased a one-acre lot on the southwest corner of Meigs and Franklin in November 1906, which was bounded on the south by the lot he already owned at 1020 West Hancock Avenue. See Warranty Deed from James J. Strickland to T. J. Epps, dated 7 November 1906, Clarke County,

Clerk of Superior Court's Office, Athens, Georgia, Book 2, page 200. Ben's parents lived at this location for the rest of their lives. (The Deed Index for Clarke County has no entry for T. J. Epps's earlier acquisition of the 1020 West Hancock Avenue lot.) *Athens* (GA) *City Directory*, 1909, lists Ben T. Epps living with his parents at 1020 West Hancock Avenue.

[14] *Athens* (GA) *City Directory*, 1909. Lists Zumpt living with his father, J. A., and stepmother, Alice Huff, at 280 Baxter Street.

[15] Tom D. Crouch, *The Bishop's Boys: A Life of Wilbur and Orville Wright* (New York: W. W. Norton & Co., 2003). The Wright brothers opened their bicycle repair and sales shop in 1892 in the midst of the national bicycle craze and began manufacturing their own brand in 1896. They used this venture to fund their interest in flight.

[16] Framed collage of five photographs and typed notes put together by Zumpt A. Huff, circa 1970; notes typed under photograph of plane number one. (This collage is hereafter referred to as "Zumpt's Collage.") Zumpt assigned each plane in his collage a number according to the order in which it was built. Zumpt's notes state that work on plane number one began in "Jan. 1908," but this same photograph is in Zumpt's scrapbook, and on the top border of this photograph there is a handwritten notation that reads, "1909 started 1908." Ben did not have his garage in January 1908 and it is unlikely that work would have started before they had a garage to build in.

[17] Elmer E. Burns, "How the Wright Airship is Kept Afloat," *Popular Mechanics*, 11/3 (March 1909): 218; George O. Squier, "Recent Progress in Aeronautics," *Science*, 29/738 (19 February 1909): 281.

[18] Galt, "Epps," *Georgia Biography*, 293.

[19] Tom Dunkin, "Ben Epps—Georgia's Pioneer in the Sky," *Atlanta Journal & Constitution*, 31 July 1966, 1-C. According to the article, this information was provided to the author by Ben's sister, Mattie Mozelle Epps Smith (Mrs. Allen G. Smith).

[20] "Two Athens Boys Building Airship," *Athens* (GA) *Banner*, 14 May 1909, 3. The photograph that was taken of this biplane on 13 May 1909 did not accompany this article and was not published in a newspaper until the 1960s.

[21] "Glenn H. Curtiss—100 Years Ago," Glenn H. Curtiss Museum, Hammondsport, New York, accessed 4 August 2015, http://www.glennhcurtissmuseum.org/educational/glenn_curtiss.html.

[22] Ibid.

[23] Ibid.

[24] Zumpt's Collage, notes typed on photograph of plane number four and notes typed on back of photograph of plane number two.

[25] "The Northeast Georgia Fair to Be Held in Athens October 5th–10th Will Be the Greatest Agricultural Fair Ever Held in This Section," *Athens* (GA) *Daily & Weekly Banner, Fair Edition*, 30 August 1903, 33. Nine Georgia counties participated in the Northeast Georgia Fair: Clarke, Oglethorpe, Oconee, Madison, Jackson, Franklin, Greene, Morgan, and Walton.

[26] Paul J. Halyard, interview with author, 24 January 2009. Paul J. Halyard is the husband of Mary Jane Halyard, granddaughter of Zumpt Huff.

[27] E-M-F Automobile Homepage, accessed 4 August 2015, http://www.emfauto.org/EMF_history.php. In 1909 Studebaker-E.M.F. manufactured 7,906 automobiles, ranking behind Ford (17,711), Buick (14,606), and Maxwell (9,460). In 1911 the company moved up to the number two manufacturer, with Ford still in the number one spot.

[28] Zumpt's Collage, notes typed on back of photograph of plane number two.

[29] "New Military Company of This City Fully Organized," *Athens* (GA) *Weekly Banner*, 9 July 1909, 1. Ben is listed as recruit No. 16 and Zumpt as No. 23. "Clarke Rifles, That Is the Name of the New Company," *Athens* (GA) *Weekly Banner*, 16 July 1909, 1. In November 1909, the Clarke Rifles acted as an escort for President William Howard Taft in Augusta, Georgia, as his car left the Georgia-Carolina Fair and traveled to the train station. "The Rifles," *Athens* (GA) *Banner*, 10 November 1909, 1. Neither Ben nor Zumpt stayed with this company for long. They are not noted in the list of men who went off to summer camp in the years that followed.

Chapter 3

[1] Zumpt's Collage, typed caption appearing below the photograph of plane number one. Incorporated in 1903, Ford Motor Company, like other United States automobile companies, entered the aviation business during World War I building Liberty airplane engines. After the war, the company returned to auto manufacturing until 1925 when it acquired the Stout Metal Airplane Company. Ford's most successful aircraft was the Ford 4AT Tri-Motor, often called the "Tin Goose" because of its corrugated metal construction. See Ford Richardson Bryan, *Beyond the Model T, The Other Ventures of Henry Ford* (Detroit, MI: Wayne State University Press, 1997).

---

[2] David L. Lewis, *The Public Image of Henry Ford, an American Folk Hero and His Company* (Detroit, MI: Wayne State University Press, 1987) 168; Russ Banham, *The Ford Country: Ford Motor Company and the Innovations That Shaped the World* (New York: Artisan, 2002) 50.

[3] *Atlanta City Directory*, 1908. Walthour & Hood's bicycle shop was located at 19 S. Forsyth Street, Atlanta.

[4] Andrew M. Homan, *Life in the Slipstream, The Legend of Bobby Walthour, Sr.* (Dulles, VA: Potomac Books, 2011) xiii, 6.

[5] Buck Peacock, "Thrills and Spills" (1999), accessed 4 August 2015, www.oldbike.com/Walthour.html. The fall 1899 race in the Piedmont Coliseum was a race between two motorcycles followed by two bicycle riders whipping around a sixth of a mile, heavily banked, bowl-shaped, wooden track at a high rate of speed. The sold-out crowd screamed with excitement as they watched through thick cigar and exhaust smoke amid a deafening noise. Bobby lost this race, but his fortune would quickly change. Ibid.

[6] *The Washington Post* listed the injuries that Bobby Walthour suffered during his cycling career: "He has broken his right collar bone 27 times; broken his left collar bone 18 times; suffered rib fractures 30 times; has had more than 40 stitches taken in both legs; has more than 100 body scars as the result of bruises; he has about 60 stitch marks in his face, forehead, and head as the result of sewed-up wounds; has broken six of the ten fingers on his hands; has been pronounced dead twice and 'fatally injured' at least six times." He was in more than 250 spills but never broke a leg, "'If I had, my career would have ended.'" *The Washington Post*, "Bike Racer Memento of 18 Years in Game," 22 August 1915, 4.

[7] Homan, *Walthour*, 6–7, 31, 115.

[8] Peacock, "Bobby Walthour, Sr.," accessed 4 August 2015, www.oldbike.com/Walthour.html.

[9] Ibid. Bobby Walthour, Sr., is enshrined in the Georgia Sports Hall of Fame, Macon, Georgia; the New York Sports Hall of Fame; and the U.S. Bicycling Hall of Fame in New Jersey.

[10] Several months prior to the race, Palmer Walthour was having his mail sent to Athens. A notice appeared in the paper listing the names of individuals, including Palmer Walthour, who had letters at the post office that had not been picked up for the week ending 23 June 1903. "Letter List," *Athens* (GA) *Banner*, 23 June 1909, 4.

[11] "Central Railway Will Push Fair," *Athens* (GA) *Banner*, 10 September 1903, 1.

12 British Anzani Co. Anzani History Page, "Alessandro Anzani—a life," accessed 4 August 2015, http://www.britishanzani.co.uk/AnzHist.htm
13 Ibid.
14 Mark Daniels, "Anzani," accessed 24 February 2009, www.icenicam.ukfsn.org/-articles1/art0019.html. Anzani also won the world championship with his motorcycle and engine at Ostend, Belgium, in 1906. Ibid.
15 Homan, *Walthour*, 174; "Bobby Buys New Motors," *Atlanta Constitution*, 12 November 1905, 8D.
16 Ibid., 174–75, citing "Au Velodrome D'Hiver," *Les Sports*, 13 November 1905; "Bobby Walthour Now in Gotham, Will Return to Atlanta Next Friday Afternoon," *Atlanta Constitution*, 26 November 1905, 4C.
17 Ibid., 176–77.
18 *Atlanta City Directory*, 1908.
19 Homan, *Walthour*, 200–201.
20 Zumpt's Collage, typed notes under photograph of plane number four.

Chapter 4
1 Ibid.
2 "The Birth of Aviation in Athens," *Athens* (GA) *Banner-Herald*, 4 August 1929, 1.
3 Valco Lyle, "Georgia's Aviation Family," *Atlanta Constitution Magazine*, 6 July 1930, 7.
4 "Occupants of the New Southern Mutual Building. Occupants Now Moving In," *Athens* (GA) *Banner*, 26 June 1908, 1.
5 "Lively Patronage at the Georgian," *Athens* (GA) *Banner*, 3 March 1909, 1.
6 Zumpt's Collage, typed notes on back of photograph of plane number two.
7 "Paving Washington Street," *Athens* (GA) *Weekly Banner*, 5 October 1906, 3.
8 "Paving of Streets Will Be Begun Very Soon," *Athens* (GA) *Daily Herald*, 6 March 1917, 1.
9 "Too Much Mud," *Athens* (GA) *Daily Herald*, 15 March 1917, 1.
10 The Confederate Monument, the second erected in the state of Georgia, was finished and dedicated on 5 May 1874. In fall 1912, in response to an increased number of accidents caused by its location, the

monument was relocated at the end of a narrow park on Broad Street near the head of College Avenue. This remains the location of the monument today, although the "narrow park" is now all concrete. "Confederate Monument," *North-East Georgian* (Athens, GA), 25 February 1874, 3; "Cost $4,444.44 Did the Second Confederate Monument in State," *Athens* (GA) *Banner*, 5 October 1912, 1.

[11] Zumpt's Collage, typed narrative on back of photograph of plane number two.

[12] Ibid.

[13] Ibid.

[14] Ibid., notes written in pencil on back of photograph of plane number two.

[15] Ibid., caption typed under photograph of plane number two. Zumpt also noted in this typed caption that they were "unable to get this monoplane off the ground." This plane's ability to fly was also analyzed by Thomas J. Benson, senior aerospace engineer, Inlets and Nozzles Branch, for the National Aeronautics and Space Administration's (NASA) Glenn Research Center in Cleveland, where he has worked for more than three decades. Benson is an expert in the field of aerodynamics and a student of history, with a particular interest in the Wright brothers and the invention of the airplane. He has traveled the country playing the part of Wilbur Wright, with Roger Storm as Orville, telling the Wright brothers' story "in first person." He built the web site, "Re-Living the Wright Way," at www.grc.nasa.gov/www/Wright/index.htm, and also built a simulator of the Wrights' 1901 wind tunnel. Benson compared the construction of the 1909 Epps-Huff II Monoplane with the 1903 Wright Flyer and performed an analysis using aerodynamic principles to determine whether the 1909 Epps-Huff II Monoplane was capable of flight. His conclusion, "[The Epps-Huff II] could not generate enough thrust with its single propeller to sustain level flight." (Correspondence: e-mail message to author, 17 December 2008 and 25 February 2009.)

Chapter 5

[1] Frances Taliaferro Thomas, *A Portrait of Historic Athens and Clarke County* (Athens: University of Georgia Press, 1992).

[2] Clarke County, Clerk of Superior Courts Office, Athens, Georgia, Deed Book 1, pages 580–81. Plat of "Lynwood Park, Athens, GA," 22 June 1906, J. W. Barnett, Engineer. The boundaries of Lynwood Park as reflected

on this plat differ from the street layout in 1909, which differs from the present-day street layout. In 1909 Lynwood Park was bounded by Cobb Street on the north, Billups Street on the east, Hancock Avenue (which became Phinizy Street at the intersection with Rocksprings) on the south, and Clover Street on the west. Today, the location of the former Lynwood Park would be bounded by Cobb Street on the north, Billups Street on the east, and Hancock Avenue on the south. Hillcrest Avenue forms the western boundary, which begins at Cobb, but today Hillcrest Avenue curves in the opposite direction that Clover Street curved in 1909, so there is no street today along what would have been the western boundary. The Plaza Street does exist today and is in the approximate location of The Plaza shown on the 1906 plat. It runs south from Hill Street but is not the entrance to a park, and although it is wider than other streets in the area, its two lanes are not separated by a traffic island as shown on the 1906 plat.

[3] Bob Fort, "Athens' Ben Epps," *Athens* (GA) *Banner-Herald & Daily News*, 19 January 1969, 8D–9D.

[4] The projected flight path would have been approximately along The Plaza, as it is located today.

[5] "Flight Is Made By Georgia Man," *Atlanta Constitution*, 30 August 1909, 3.

[6] Ibid.

[7] Zumpt's Collage, typed caption under photograph of plane number three.

[8] *Atlanta Constitution*, "Flight Is Made By Georgia Man," 30 August 1909, 3.

[9] "Louis Blériot," National Aeronautics and Space Administration, U.S. Centennial of Flight Commission, accessed 19 September 2012: www.centennialofflight.gov/essay/Dictionary/Bleriot/DI11.htm; "Louis Blériot Biography," accessed 1 August 2015: www.biographybase.com/biography/Bleriot_Louis.html; Montash College, "The Pioneers," s.v. "Louis Blériot," accessed 1 August 2015: www.ctie.monash.edu.au/hargrave/bleriot.html. The Blériot V made its first successful flight on 5 April 1907. After a 100-m (305-ft) run, the machine briefly left the ground. The Blériot V was destroyed in a crash on 19 April 1907.

[10] "Georgians Make Flight in a New Aeroplane," *Atlanta Georgian & News*, 30 August 1909, 3.

---

[11] "Two Athens Boys Invent Aeroplane," *Augusta* (GA) *Chronicle*, 30 August 1909, 1.

[12] "Short Flight of Georgia Monoplane," *Savannah* (GA) *Morning News*, 30 August 1909, 1.

[13] "Georgia Aeroplane Failed to Work," *Macon* (GA) *News*, 31 August 1909, 1. This article chronicled the second attempt at flight by the monoplane on Monday, 30 August, but also gave details of the first flight.

[14] "Didn't Fly Very Far," *Valdosta* (GA) *Times*, 30 August 1909, 3.

[15] "Georgia Has an Aeroplane Flight," *Charlotte* (NC) *Observer*, 30 August 1909; "First Flight in Georgia," *Grand Rapids* (MI) *Press*, 30 August 1909.

[16] *Athens* (GA) *Weekly Banner*, 3 September 1909, 4, column 1.

[17] "Funeral Notices," *Athens* (GA) *Banner-Herald*, 18 October 1937. Ben had been a long-time member of First Baptist Church, Athens, Georgia, at the time of his death. "Death Notices," *Florida Times Union* (Jacksonville), 25 November 1925, B7. Zumpt had been a long-time member of the First United Methodist Church, Jacksonville, Florida, at the time of his death.

[18] "Athens Machine Fails to Fly," *Atlanta Constitution*, 31 August 1909, 1.

[19] "Flying Machine Near Lexington," *Oglethorpe Echo*, (Lexington, GA) 3 September 1909, 1. "Henry Walden," Aeroflies, Capsule Biographies, accessed 3 August 2015, http://www.aeroflies.com/bio_w.html.

[20] "Obituaries," *New York Times*, 14 September 1964.

[21] Aerofiles, Capsule Biographies, "Henry Walden," http://www.aerofiles.com/bio_w.html.

[22] Ibid.; Joshua Stoff, *Images of America, Long Island Aircraft Crashes, 1909–1959* (New York: Arcadia Publishing, 2004). A photograph of Dr. Henry W. Walden's Walden III is on page 11.

[23] Aeroflies, Capsule Biographies, "Henry Walden," accessed 3 August 2015, http://www.aeroflies.com/bio_w.html; National Aviation Hall of Fame, "Walden, Henry W.," accessed 3 August 2015, http://www.nationalaviation.org/walden-henry/.

[24] "Falls With New Monoplane," *New York Times*, 4 August 1910, 2. This article mistakenly refers to the pilot of the monoplane as "Dr. Charles F. Walden, a New York dentist." There was no dentist in Manhattan by this name. The article apparently confused Dr. Henry Walden with another aviator and member of the Aeronautic Society of New York at the time

whose name was Charles F. Willard. Willard, a Harvard graduate, was a racecar driver and Glenn Curtiss's first student pilot.

[25] Aerofiles, "Henry Walden."

[26] Ibid.

[27] "History of the Early Birds of Aviation," accessed 3 August 2015, Early Aviators, http://earlyaviators.com/ehistory.htm.

[28] Ibid. This site has a photograph of Henry Walden receiving his plaque at the 4 December 1959 meeting.

Chapter 6

[1] Lola Trammell, "Man Who Put Georgia in the Air," *Atlanta Journal Magazine*, 27 March 1949, 8.

[2] Thomas W. Reed, "Echoes from Memoryland, The Late Ben Epps and the Flying Machine He Built," *Athens* (GA) *Banner-Herald*, 1 March 1949, 4.

[3] Ibid.

[4] The Works Progress Administration, later known as the Work Projects Administration, was a Federal program established during the Great Depression to keep people off charity. A part of the writers' program involved the creation and compilation of some 2,900 "Life Histories" to collect and preserve folklore and prepare social and ethnic studies. Each state had a writers' project. In Georgia there were nine regions. Clarke County was in region 6, and all of the interviewers in Athens were women. Mrs. Sadie B. Hornsby conducted the interview of Omie Epps on 6 March 1939 at Omie's home. See Sadie B. Hornsby, "An Air-Minded Family," *Athens Memories, The WPA Federal Writers' Project Interviews*, ed. Al Hester (Athens, GA: The Green Berry Press, 2001) 13–29.

[5] Ibid., 23. A digital version of Sadie Hornsby's original, typed, and unedited interview with Omie Epps can be viewed at Library of Congress, American Life Histories: Manuscripts from the Federal Writers' Project, 1936–1940, "An Air-Minded Family," accessed 4 August 2015: http://www.loc.gov/item/wpalh000513/

[6] Ibid., 20.

[7] "Georgians Make Flight in a New Aeroplane," *Atlanta Georgian & News*, 30 August 1909, 3.

[8] Ibid. Both Reed and the *Atlanta Georgian & News* article agreed on how far the Epps-Huff III Monoplane traveled on this successful private trial. As quoted, Reed said it was "about one hundred yards" and the *Atlanta*

Georgian & News article said it traveled "a distance of 300 feet," ten times the distance the Walden III Monoplane traveled 106 days later and claimed the record for being the first monoplane to fly in the United States.

Chapter 7

[1] "Building Track for Monoplane," *Atlanta Georgian & News*, 2 September 1909, 2.

[2] Ibid.

[3] "Monoplane Is Built by Georgia Aviator," *Atlanta Georgian & News*, 3 January 1910, 2.

[4] Ibid.

[5] "Aeroplane Tested on City Streets," *Athens* (GA) *Banner*, 1 January 1910, 1.

[6] "Benj. Epps of Athens Improving Aeroplane," *Athens* (GA) *Banner*, 7 January 1910, 6. Newspaper articles written about Ben and Zumpt often incorrectly spelled Ben's surname as "Eppes" and Zumpt's forename as "Zump," but this is the only article that refers to Zumpt as "Zumphrey."

[7] Ibid.

[8] "Aeroplane Tested Yesterday Carried to County on Dray," *Athens* (GA) *Banner*, 24 February 1910, 8.

Chapter 8

[1] "Blériot, Louis," National Aeronautics and Space Administration, U.S. Centennial of Flight Commission, accessed 19 September 2012, http://www.centennialofflight.gov/essay/Dictionary/Bleriot/DI11.htm; "Blériot, Louis," accessed 1 August 2015, http://www.biographybase.com/biography/Bleriot_Louis.html.

[2] Ibid.

[3] Ibid.

[4] Zumpt Huff's scrapbook of photographs is in the possession of his granddaughter, Mary Jane Halyard (hereafter cited as "Zumpt's Scrapbook"). This notation is typed in the scrapbook under the photograph. This same photograph is in Ben's scrapbook (Image Number 15), Epps Papers, Hargrett Library, Epps's Scrapbook, 12. There are four photographs on this page. A typed notation in the center of the page identifies one of the photographs as being a plane "built by Ben T. Epps," and the planes in the other three photographs, including the photograph of the Blériot XI, as

"unknown." Ben would have known this was a photograph of the Blériot XI and would not have typed this incorrect notation.

⁵ Mark Daniels, "Anzani," accessed 24 February 2009, www.icenicam.ukfsn.org/-articles1/art0019.html.

⁶ Zumpt's Collage, notes typed on back of photograph of plane number two.

⁷ "Half Mile Racetrack for Athens Is Nearly Completed," *Athens* (GA) *Banner*, 26 April 1910, 6. The Davis-Escoe track derived its name from the proprietors, Fred L. Davis and W. Y. Escoe. Their investment in the track was reported to be more than $5,000.

⁸ "Races Were Most Successful Yesterday at Davis-Esco [*sic*] Track," *Athens* (GA) *Weekly Banner*, 1 July 1910, 2.

⁹ Ibid. This article also reported, "One moneyed man has enough confidence in the invention to grant to young Epps a fair monthly bonus while he is working on the perfection of the machine." This is the only mention of any potential third-party financial backing in the Epps-Huff partnership or in any of Ben Epps's subsequent airplane-building ventures. Although mentioned in this article, there is no evidence that the Epps-Huff partnership or Ben Epps, individually, ever received any financial backing.

¹⁰ Epps Papers, Hargrett Library, Epps's Scrapbook, 4.

¹¹ Zumpt's Scrapbook.

¹² Epps Papers, Hargrett Library, Epps's Scrapbook, 4.

¹³ Zumpt's Collage, notes typed on front of photograph of plane number four (Image Number 18).

¹⁴ Epps Papers, Hargrett Library, Epps's Scrapbook, 2.

¹⁵ Advertisement, *Athens* (GA) *Banner*, 1 December 1910, 5. "Michelin Tires, In Stock by Epps Garage, 392 Washington Street."

¹⁶ *Atlanta City Directory*, 1911. Zumpt is listed as residing at 163 Marietta Street, Atlanta, Georgia.

¹⁷ According to Ben Epps, Jr., his father "put all his time and money into airplanes. Airplanes cost him more than he ever made from them." "Ben Epps: Athenian Was Pioneer Georgia Aviator," *Athens* (GA) *Banner-Herald & Daily News*, 29 February 1976, 12G.

¹⁸ Victor Zarnowitz, *Business Cycles: Theory, History, Indicators and Forecasting* (Chicago: University of Chicago Press, 1996). According to Zarnowitz, business activity decreased by 14.7 percent during this two-year recession.

[19] *Our Family Tree, Ficquett-Wilbanks-Huff, Extended Families, 1788–1995,* ed. Thora O. Kimsey (Monroe, GA: Thora O. Kimsey, 1995) 158. Floy worked in an ice cream parlor in Athens.

[20] "Flatwoods," *Oglethorpe Echo,* (Lexington, GA) 5 November 1909, 10.

[21] "Ben Epps Flying Machine Inventor Ran Over a Rabbit on Road in Auto," *Athens* (GA) *Weekly Banner,* 3 March 1911, 2.

[22] "Broke Arm Sunday While Cranking Another Man's Machine for Him," *Athens* (GA) *Banner,* 11 September 1911, 8.

[23] In an interview after his death, his widow said, "Ben was never a person to talk about himself. He always brought clippings home for me to read." Sadie B. Hornsby, "An Air-Minded Family," *Athens Memories, The WPA Federal Writers' Project Interviews,* ed. Al Hester (Athens, GA: The Green Berry Press, 2001) 21.

[24] "Benj. Eppes of Athens Improving Aeroplane," *Athens* (GA) *Banner,* 7 January 1910, 6.

[25] "The Birth of Aviation in Athens...Twenty Years Ago," *Athens* (GA) *Banner-Herald,* 4 August 1929, 1.

[26] Hugh Rowe, *History of Athens and Clarke County* (1923; repr., Greenville, SC: Southern Historical Press, 2000).

[27] "Ben Epps Dies Last Night of Plane Crash Injuries Sustained Here Saturday," *Athens* (GA) *Banner-Herald,* 17 October 1937, 1.

[28] "Death Finally Overtakes Pioneer Georgia Aviator," *Athens* (GA) *Banner-Herald,* 19 October 1937, 2.

[29] "Funeral Notices," *Athens* (GA) *Banner-Herald,* 18 October 1937; "Funeral Rites for Ben T. Epps Today, Companion Serious," *Athens* (GA) *Banner-Herald,* 18 October 1937, 1.

[30] "Echoes from the Past, 75 Years Ago, September 3, 1909," *Oglethorpe Echo,* (Lexington, GA) 6 September 1984, 4.

[31] Ibid.

Chapter 9
[1] *Atlanta City Directory,* 1911. Zumpt's residence is listed as 163 Marietta Street and lists the location of A La Mode Theatre as 30 Whitehall Street.

[2] *Atlanta City Directory,* 1912. Zumpt's residence is listed as 182 W. Merritts Avenue. The Majestic Theatre is listed at 30 Peachtree Street.

[3] *Atlanta City Directory*, 1913. Zumpt's residence is listed as 17 Jonesboro Drive. There is no listing for his occupation.

[4] *Atlanta City Directory*, 1914. Zumpt's residence is listed as 15 Houston Street. The Montgomery Theater is listed at 162 Auburn Avenue.

[5] *Atlanta City Directory*, 1915. The directory lists Zumpt as boarding at 62 Walton Street. There is no street address given for Alamo Theater No. 2.

[6] *Our Family Tree, Ficquett-Wilbanks-Huff, Extended Families, 1788–1995*, ed. Thora O. Kimsey (Monroe, GA: Thora O. Kimsey, 1995) 157; *Athens* (GA) *City Directory*, 1909, James Huff's occupation is listed as medicine vendor.

[7] *Our Family Tree*, 171.

[8] *Atlanta City Directory*, 1916.

[9] *Our Family Tree*, 171.

[10] Ibid., 158; "Funeral of Mr. Huff at Cartersville [*sic*]," *Athens* (GA) *Banner-Herald*, 10 April 1917, 8. James Huff is buried next to his first wife, Annabel, in the cemetery behind Carnesville United Methodist Church in Carnesville, Georgia.

[11] *Our Family Tree*, 158. Alice remained in Atlanta the rest of her life. She died on 2 March 1951 at the age of seventy-seven. See "Funeral Notices, Huff," *Atlanta Constitution*, 3 March 1951.

[12] "U.S. Is Now at War! Wilson Placed His Signature to War Declaration Today," *Atlanta Journal*, 6 April 1917, 1.

[13] Jennifer D. Keen, *World War I* (Westport, CT: Greenwood Press, 2006) 35–36.

[14] Franklin M. Garrett, *Atlanta and Environs*, vol. 2 (1954; repr., Athens: University of Georgia Press, 1969) 717.

[15] Keen, *World War I*, 35–36. Eventually, 24 million men registered for the draft. Over 65 percent of those who registered received deferments or exemptions from service; 43 percent of deferments went to married men who were the sole providers of families.

[16] Ibid.

[17] Garrett, *Atlanta and Environs*, 749, citing, Walter G. Cooper, *Story of Georgia*, vol. 3 (New York: American Historical Society, 1938) 465–66.

[18] *Our Family Tree*, 171.

[19] A formal state of war between the two sides persisted for another seven months until the signing of the Treaty of Versailles with Germany on 28 June 1919.

[20] *Atlanta City Directory*, 1925. Zumpt's residence is listed as 55A Clarke Street.

[21] *Atlanta City of Directory*, 1926. Zumpt's residence is listed as 402 Stewart Avenue. (Stewart Avenue is now named Metropolitan Parkway.)

[22] Mary Jane Halyard, interview with author, 24 January 2009.

[23] Ibid.; "Death Notices, Huff," *Florida Times-Union*, 25 November 1975, B-7.

[24] Ibid.

[25] Ibid.; see also *Our Family Tree*, 172. The house that Zumpt built was located at 1543 6th Avenue North, Jacksonville Beach, Florida.

[26] *Our Family Tree*, 173.

[27] Ibid.

[28] Ibid, 173–74; Mary Jane Halyard, interview with author, 24 January 2009.

[29] John Pennington, "Ben Epps's 1912 Monoplane," *Atlanta Journal & Constitution Magazine*, 7 July 1968, 8.

[30] A photograph of the 1912 monoplane replica in front of an Epps Air Service hangar can be seen at Epps Aviation, "About Us," "Timeline of History," "1968," accessed 6 August 2015, www.eppsaviation.com.

[31] Epps Papers, Hargrett Library, Box 1, Folder 1:3, Letters, Receipts. Bill to Zumpt from Smithway Studios, West Somerville, Massachusetts, dated 17 December 1968 for "one 4x5 copy negative from furnished original, three 8x10 enlargements from above negative, unmounted."

[32] Meeting at Athens Federal Savings and Loan Association, Ben T. Epps, Jr., speaker, *Athens* (GA) *Historical Society Newsletter*, 9 January 1969.

[33] *Our Family Tree*, 176. Richard N. Fickett III, president, Athens Historical Society, to Zumpt, 15 January 1969. Fickett's letter also acknowledges that Zumpt spoke at this meeting and compliments Zumpt stating, "Your [t]alk added to the knowledge of the eventful history of Mr. Ben Epps, Sr.'s development and flying of the Airplane."

[34] Bob Fort, "Athens' Ben Epps," *Athens* (GA) *Banner-Herald & Daily News*, 19 January 1969, 8D-9D.

[35] Richard N. Fickett III to Ben T. Epps, Jr., 13 January 1969, in the collection of Pat Epps.

[36] Ibid.

[37] Epps Papers, Hargrett Library, Box 1, Folder 1:3, Letters, Receipts. Ibid. Zumpt to Ben, Jr., 21 February 1969.

[38] Ibid.

[39] Zumpt's Collage, copy of article from *Athens* (GA) *Weekly Banner*, 14 May 1909, 7. Fickett wrote a note to Zumpt that accompanied this newspaper article, which reads, "Athens Georgia newspaper 'The Weekly Banner' May 14, 1909, page 7, copied by Xerox from original, at the Clarke County (Ga) Court house 1/16/1969, R. N. Fickett III." Ibid.

[40] Epps Papers, Hargrett Library, Box 1, Folder 1:3, Letters, Receipts. Ibid. Zumpt to Ben, Jr., 21 February 1969. The photograph of the plane wrecked in Lynwood Park that Zumpt references is the one in Image Number 11. The typed note that Zumpt placed under this photograph in his collage states, "The monoplne [*sic*] was an improved model of the monoplane. It was carried to Lynnwood Park for a trial flight, this was airplane #3 and the photograph is #3 plane. In its first attempt it refused to obey the control levers, veered to the right at the second terrace, and there it had [*sic*] butted into a barbed wire fence. It was carried back to the lot on Lumpkin Street where plane number 4 was constructed from its remains." Zumpt's Collage.

[41] Ibid.

[42] Ibid. Zumpt to Smithway Studios, West Somerville, MA, 18 April 1969. "I would like for you to make an 8x10 enlargement from. Ship one negative and enlargement to me and one negative and enlargement to Ben Jr."

[43] Epps Papers, Hargrett Library, Box 1, Folder 1:7, "Epps Papers, Photographs, Ben Epps, Epps Family members & others." Photograph of Julius D. Bishop mailed by Zumpt to Ben, Jr., envelope postmarked 10 February 1970.

[44] Zumpt's Scrapbook.

[45] The existence of this typed narrative was not discovered until 2011 when this photograph was removed from the framed collage by one of Zumpt's granddaughters.

[46] Teresa Laughlin Gensheimer, email to author, 30 January 2011.

[47] A senior Special Collections librarian confirmed to the author that the library has no listing in its card file, vertical file index for either Zumpt Huff or Ben Epps. Kathleen Krizek, email to author, 3 November 2007.

[48] Epps Papers, Hargrett Library, Box 1, Folder 1:7, "Epps Papers, Photographs, Ben Epps, Epps Family members & others." Photograph of Julius D. Bishop mailed by Zumpt to Ben, Jr., envelope postmarked 10 February 1970.

[49] *Our Family Tree*, 174. Don Kimsey, son of Nell Huff and Isaac Melvin Kimsey, stated that this article appeared in the *Florida Times-Union Magazine* (Jacksonville, FL) but did not provide a date. This magazine is no longer published, but while it was, it was inserted in the Sunday edition of the paper. The Jacksonville, Florida, public library has a collection of the *Florida Times-Union* (Jacksonville, FL) newspapers during this period, but the collection is not complete, as several issues are missing. The author did search the issues that are in this collection for the period of April 1969 through November 1975 but did not find the article referenced by the nephew.

[50] "Death Notices, Huff," *Florida Times-Union*, (Jacksonville, FL) 25 November 1975, B-7.

Chapter 10

[1] Epps Family Cousins Club, accessed 5 August 2015: http://reocities.com/Heartland/oaks/4050/epps.htm.

[2] Sadie B. Hornsby, "An Air-Minded Family," *Athens Memories, The WPA Federal Writers' Project Interviews*, ed. Al Hester (Athens, GA: The Green Berry Press, 2001) 17.

[3] Ibid., 18–19.

[4] Ibid., 19.

[5] Ibid., 19–20. Omie described her first date with Ben as follows: "My friend [who introduced her to Ben] kept asking me for a date to go automobile riding. I didn't know girls went riding at night. I told my mother, she told me it would be no harm if there was another couple along. So when my friend, [Ben] and another girl came to my house I didn't know I was to be with [Ben] until he got there. From that time on we had dates regular." Ibid.

[6] "Society, Things of Interest to Women," *Athens* (GA) *Banner*, 10 September 1912, 2.

[7] Ibid.

[8] Marriage license issued to Ben Epps and Miss Omie L. Williams on 5 December 1913; married on 7 December 1913. Clarke County marriage records, Clerk of Probate Court's Office, Athens, Georgia, Book M, 1909–1917, 302.

[9] Epps Family Cousins Club, accessed 5 August 2015: http://reocities.com/Heartland/oaks/4050/epps.htm.

[10] Hornsby, "Air-Minded Family," *Athens Memories*, 20.

[11] "In Society," *Athens* (GA) *Banner*, 26 November 1914, 2. "Mrs. Ben Eppes [*sic*] and little daughter, Evelyn, are visiting in Siloam."

[12] Hornsby, "Air-Minded Family," *Athens Memories*, 20.

[13] Ibid.

[14] *Online Etymology Dictionary*, s.v. "aileron," accessed 4 August 2015, http://www.etymonline.com/index.php?search=aileron.

[15] National Aeronautics and Space Administration, Glenn Research Center, accessed 4 August 2015, http://www.grc.nasa.gov/WWW/k-12/airplane/air.html.

[16] Tom Crouch, "Oldies and Oddities; Where Do Ailerons Come From?" *Air & Space Smithsonian Magazine*, 24/2 (September 2009): 12; Joe Yoon, "Origins of Control Surfaces," accessed 4 August 2015, http://www.aerospaceweb.org/question/history/q0103.shtml.

[17] Ibid.

[18] Ibid.

[19] Yoon, "Control Surfaces," aerospaceweb.org.

[20] Tom Dunkin, "Ben Epps," *Atlanta Journal & Constitution*, 31 July 1966, 1-C.

[21] John Pennington, "Ben Epps's 1912 Monoplane," *Atlanta Journal & Constitution Magazine*, 7 July 1968, 8.

[22] Epps Papers, Hargrett Library, Epps's Scrapbook, 20, note written on black scrapbook paper.

[23] Ibid.

[24] "Classic Clippings, New Aeroplane Wrecked," *Athens* (GA) *Daily Herald*, 26 August 1915, 6.

[25] "Athens Big Auto Show to Be Feature of Big Feature-Month, Scores of Cars to Be on Exhibition—Flying Machine to Be Interesting Exhibit," *Athens* (GA) *Banner*, 11 May 1916, 1.

[26] "Flying Machine," *Athens* (GA) *Banner*, 18 May 1916, 22.

[27] "Ben Epps," *Athens* (GA) *Banner-Herald & Daily News*, 29 February 1976, 12G.

[28] "News of Society, Social Items," *Athens* (GA) *Daily Herald*, 28 June 1916, 3.

[29] Warranty Deed from Thomas J. Epps to Ben T. Epps, 13 November 1917, Clarke County, Clerk of Superior Court's Office, Athens, Georgia, Deed Book 21, page 554.

[30] By Act of 1815, the corporate limit of the town of Athens was extended to one mile in every direction from the college chapel. By Act of

1872, the General Assembly amended the charter of the town of Athens, making it a city and extending its authority and jurisdiction a distance of two miles in every direction from the college chapel. See *North-East Georgia*, 24 February 1875, 1, publishing the State Supreme Court's decision in *John S. Linton v. Mayor and Council of Athens*, decided on 9 February 1875.

[31] Hornsby, "Air-Minded Family," *Athens Memories*, 6.

[32] Hargrett, Epps Papers 1:12 Writings—Reminiscences of Ben Epps, Jr., #2. Ben, Jr., also recalled that when he went to his grandfather's store, which was next to a pecan orchard, his grandfather would give him a stick of peppermint candy. The store sold flour, meal, tobacco, and "just the normal things a small county store would handle." Later, his grandfather built a corn mill on the side of the store.

[33] Hargrett, Epps Papers, Box 5, Folder 5:3, Ben Epps Project 2001: Interview of Virginia "Jenny" Epps Whitaker, Ben's daughter.

[34] Ibid.

[35] "106 of Clarke's Quota of 181 Men are Certified, 20 More Claims for Exemption," *Athens* (GA) *Banner*, 24 August 1917, 6.

[36] "Names and Numbers of Men Registered in Clarke County," *Athens* (GA) *Daily Herald*, 10 July 1917, 2.

[37] "Selection of Men Made for New Army," *Athens* (GA) *Daily Herald*, 20 July 1917, 1. The name of the registrant of the first number drawn in Clarke County was Julian Erwin.

[38] See "More Than Half of Clarke's Quota of Men Under Frist Call Are Already in Sight," *Athens* (GA) *Banner Weekly*, 10 August 1917, 2; "Clarke Board has Certified 265 Men to District Board," *Athens* (GA) *Banner Weekly*, 14 September 1917, 3.

[39] "How Exemption Under the Draft Act Will Be Claimed," *Athens* (GA) *Banner*, 12 July 1917, 5.

[40] "Complete List of Athens and Clarke County Boys Who Served in World War," *Athens* (GA) *Daily Herald*, 30 June 1922, 13.

[41] Georgia Historical Marker No. 029-16, "Georgia's Pioneer Aviator, Ben T. Epps, 1888–1937," at Athens-Clarke County-Ben Epps Airport, Athens-Clarke County, Georgia/Erected 1987.

[42] Peachstate Aerodrome, "Candler Field Museum History," accessed 1 August 2015, www.peachstateaero.com/museum/. In 1919, James H. Elliott leased the old Atlanta Speedway near Hapeville, Georgia, and cleared a 3.5-acre area that could be used for aircraft operations. In fall 1919 he opened his flying business at the field.

43 "Notice," *Athens* (GA) *Banner*, 10 February 1918, 12.

44 "Ben Epps," *Athens* (GA) *Banner-Herald &Daily News*, 29 February 1976, 12G.

45 Hornsby, "Air-Minded Family," *Athens Memories*, 25. See also "Ben Epps," *Athens* (GA) *Banner-Herald & Daily News*, 29 February 1976, 12G.

46 Military Factory, "Aeromarine 40 Flying Boat (1918)," accessed 4 August 2015, http://www.militaryfactory.com/aircraft/detail.asp?aircraft_id=713.

47 "The News of the Week," *Aerial Age Weekly*, 2/4 (11 October 1915): 80.

48 Paul Poberezny, "Doug Rolfe and His JN–D–4," *Sport Aviation*, 9/12, (December 1960): 23. Douglas Percy Rolfe was Monte Rolfe's brother. Both were born in London, Monte in 1894 and Doug in 1896.

49 Hornsby, "Air-Minded Family," *Athens Memories*, 25.

50 Ibid.

51 "Advertising and Passenger Plane Firm in Athens," *Athens* (GA) *Weekly Banner*, 21 November 1919, 3.

52 "Air 'Taxi' Service Planned to Start Here in October," *Athens* (GA) *Weekly Banner*, 22 August 1919, 3.

53 Frederick Allen, *Atlanta Rising: The Invention of an International City 1946–1996* (Atlanta: Longstreet Press, 1996) 21; Peachstate Aerodrome, "Candler Field Museum History," accessed 1 August 2015, www.peachstateaero.com/museum/; Franklin M. Garrett, *Atlanta and Environs*, vol. 2 (1954; repr., Athens: University of Georgia Press, 1969) 733, 811, 851. On 16 April 1925, the City of Atlanta and Candler signed the lease giving Atlanta its first airfield. The city subsequently purchased the property from Candler on 13 April 1929 for $94,500.

54 "Air 'Taxi' Service Planned to Start Here in October," *Athens* (GA) *Weekly Banner*, 22 August 1919, 3.

55 "Legal Ad/Notice of Incorporation," *Athens* (GA) *Banner*, 25 June 1920, 8. In addition to Ben T. Epps and Louis Montague Rolfe, Blanton Fortson is listed as a third incorporator of the company. Fortson was a local Athens attorney.

56 "Advertising and Passenger Plane Firm in Athens," *Athens* (GA) *Weekly Banner*, 21 November 1919, 3.

57 *Athens* (GA) *City Directory*, 1920–1921. Lists Rolfe's occupation as "aviator" living with his wife, Florence, at 140 Barber Street.

58 Poberezny, "Doug Rolfe," 23.

[59] "Advertising and Passenger Plane Firm in Athens," *Athens* (GA) *Weekly Banner*, 21 November 1919, 3.

[60] Ibid. E. H. Dorsey, Jr., was reported to be the first passenger to ride on the converted seaplane.

[61] Advertisement, *Athens* (GA) *Banner*, 8 February 1920, 10.

[62] "Will Stage All of the Latest Thrills," *Athens* (GA) *Banner*, 23 January 1920, 1.

[63] "Aviators and Airplane Acrobat Arrive for Big 'Air Exhibition,'" *Athens* (GA) *Banner Weekly*, 13 February 1920, 1.

[64] "Banner Delivered by Airplane, Copies Are Taken to Washington and Elberton," *Athens* (GA) *Banner*, 16 February 1920, 1.

[65] "Pictures of City Taken in Air by Aviator," *Athens* (GA) *Banner*, 29 January 1920, 1.

[66] Epps Papers, Hargrett Library, Epps's Scrapbook, 29; Hargrett, Epps Papers, Box 1, Folder 1:15, Photographs, Aerial Views of Athens and University of Georgia.

[67] "The H. W. Campbell United Shows," *Athens* (GA) *Banner*, 12 March 1920, 1.

[68] "Aviator Rolfe Visits Winder in Search of Flying Field," *Athens* (GA) *Banner*, 22 February 1920, 11.

[69] Advertisement, "Aeroplane,"*Athens* (GA) *Banner*, 1 August 1920, 15.

[70] "Planning to Make Airplanes Soon," *Lenoir* (NC) *News-Topic*, 20 January 1921, 1. The "Carolina Cloudster" was to be "of the enclosed limousine type, electrically started, lighted and heated, comparing favorably with machines selling for $30,000 in Europe, and to be offered at about half that sum."

[71] Paul Poberezny, "Doug Rolfe and His JN-D-4," *Sport Aviation*, 9/12 (December 1960): 23–24.

[72] Epps Papers, Hargrett Library, Epps's Scrapbook, 20.

[73] "Monte Rolfe Is Dead in Plane Smash in Cuba," *Athens* (GA) *Banner-Herald*, 24 August 1921, 3. Monte Rolfe was killed in a plane crash in Havana, Cuba, on 14 August 1921.

[74] Ibid. This article reprints Doug Rolfe's letter to the editor. It recounts several events in Monte's life including an incident at Daytona Beach, Florida, in spring 1921 when a deaf women ran in front of Monte's plane as he was landing on the beach and was killed (Monte was later acquitted of any wrongdoing by a coroner's inquiry) and that Monte had

recently taken President Warren G. Harding's daughter and some of her friends on their first airplane ride.

[75] "New Aeroplane Is in Athens," *Athens* (GA) *Banner-Herald*, 15 January 1922, 5. The article identifies Ben as the "manager of the Epps flying company." Captain A. G. Davis was the recipient of the Air Force Cross in World War I. "Honours," *Flight*, 11/2 (9 January 1919): 48.

[76] Hargrett, Epps Papers 1:12 Writings—Reminiscences of Ben Epps, Jr., #2. According to Ben, Jr., this tent was large enough to cover about three Jenny airplanes.

[77] Edwin Milton, *A History of Hapeville* (Alpharetta, GA: W. H. Wolfe Associates, 1991) 151.

[78] Image Number 31 is a picture of Ben Epps, Grover Presnell, and Doug Davis and is dated June 1922. This photograph appears three times in Ben's scrapbook. One is dated "June 1922," one is dated "1919," and the third is not dated. Based on newspaper articles placing Doug Davis in Athens in 1922, the date "June 1922" is correct. See Epps Papers, Hargrett Library, Epps's Scrapbook, 21 ("1919"), 42 ("June 1922"), and 98 (undated).

[79] "Davis, Douglas H.," Georgia Aviation Hall of Fame, Century of Flight Hangar, Museum of Aviation, Robins Air Force Base, Warner Robins, Georgia, plaque; "Davis, Douglas H.," Georgia Aviation Hall of Fame, accessed 1 August 2015, http://www.gaaviationhalloffame.com/Hall-of-Fame.48.0.html?avid=35; "Doug Davis," Early Birds of Aviation, accessed 4 August 2015, http://www.earlyaviators.com/edavisdo.htm, providing extracts from Edwin Milton, *A History of Hapeville* (Alpharetta, GA: W. H. Wolfe Associates, 1991).

[80] "'Mexican Dynamite,' Fox Terrier Dog, to Leap From 'Plane," *Athens* (GA) *Banner-Herald*, 9 July 1922, 1.

[81] *Ben Epps, The Legacy of Georgia's First Aviator*, DVD, written and produced by William J. Evelyn (Athens: University of Georgia, 2001).

[82] "Davis, Douglas H., " Georgia Aviation Hall of Fame, Century of Flight Hangar, Museum of Aviation, Robins Air Force Base, Warner Robins, Georgia, plaque; see also "Davis, Douglas H.," Georgia Aviation Hall of Fame, accessed 1 August 2015, http://www.gaaviationhalloffame.com/Hall-of-Fame.48.0.html?avid=35; Early Birds of Aviation, "Doug Davis," accessed 4 August 2015, http://www.earlyaviators.com/edavisdo.htm, providing extracts for Edwin Milton, *A History of Hapeville* (Alpharetta, GA: W. H. Wolfe Associates 1991). William B. Hartsfield became mayor of Atlanta in 1937. He served

from 1937–1941 and 1942–1962 and is the longest-serving mayor of Atlanta to date.

[83] "Sensational Air Stunts," *Athens* (GA) *Banner-Herald*, 22 October 1922, 7.

[84] "Athens to Be on Airplane Route, Landing Field Has Been Chosen," *Athens* (GA) *Daily Banner*, 19 December 1922, 1.

[85] Ibid.

[86] "Landing Field Has Been Chosen," *Athens* (GA) *Banner*, 20 December 1922, 1.

[87] "New Aeroplane," 5.

[88] "Athens May Soon Get Mail by Air from Washington," *Athens* (GA) *Banner-Herald*, 8 October 1922, 1.

[89] "Atlanta to Be Air Mail Stop," *Athens* (GA) *Daily Herald*, 1 December 1922, 1.

[90] Garrett, *Atlanta and Environs*, 733; see also "Air Mail Plane Leaves Atlanta for Jacksonville," *Athens* (GA) *Banner-Herald*, 15 September 1926, 1.

[91] "Air Mail—Air Express—Air Passenger Service Inaugurated Here," *Athens* (GA) *Banner-Herald*, 5 August 1949, 1; see also "Contract Air Mail First Flights AM-98," accessed 1 August 2015, http://www.aerodacious.com/ccAM098.htm. Southern Airways applied for Civil Aeronautics Board certificates to become a local air carrier in eight southern states, but World War II interrupted issuance of the certificates. The AM-98 routes were awarded to Southern Airways on 10 June 1949. The first airmail flight out of Athens was 5 August 1949. Ibid.

[92] Dan Magill, "Ten Thousand People Throng Athens Sat. for 'University Home Coming' Festivities and Merchants Trade Campaign," *Athens* (GA) *Banner-Herald*, 11 November 1923, 1.

[93] Ibid.

[94] Ibid.

[95] "A Second Flying Machine for Athens," *Athens* (GA) *Banner*, 20 January 1923, 4; "Plane and Hangar Suffer in Storm," *Athens* (GA) *Banner-Herald*, 9 March 1923, 3.

[96] Gravure Pictorial Section, *Atlanta Constitution*, 25 November 1923.

[97] Ibid.

[98] Marcus Bryant, "Old Dominion Bows to Red and Black," *Athens* (GA) *Banner-Herald*, 11 November 1923, 6.

Chapter 11

[1] Epps Papers, Hargrett Library, Epps's Scrapbook, 64. Newspaper clipping, Bill Tyus, "13-Year-Old Boy *Flies* Plane," 8 December 1929. This is most likely from the *Athens* (GA) *Banner-Herald*, but there are no issues for the month of December 1929 in the newspaper collection at the University of Georgia Library.

[2] Evelyn Epps Galt, "Epps, Benjamin Thomas," in *Dictionary of Georgia Biography*, vol. 1, eds. Kenneth Coleman and Charles Stephen Gurr (Athens: University of Georgia Press, 1983) 294. Galt says the date of this design was 1925. The drawing of this design in Epps Papers, Hargrett Library, Box 1, Folder 1:2, "Drawings," lists this model as a 1924 design. Ben's scrapbook contains a penned notation that reads, "Light monoplane built 1924." Also, newspaper clippings in Ben's scrapbook indicate that his plane was built in 1924. See Epps Papers, Hargrett Library, Epps's Scrapbook, 40, newspaper clipping dated 31 May 1925, "Midget Plane Invention of Athenian, Makes Successful Trip" and newspaper clipping dated 1 June 1925, "Big Crowd Sees 'Midget' Plane in Trial Flight." These two articles are most likely from the *Athens* (GA) *Banner-Herald*, but there are no issues of the *Athens* (GA) *Banner-Herald* for 31 May 1925 or 1 June 1925 in the newspaper collection at the University of Georgia Library for confirmation.

[3] Epps Papers, Hargrett Library, Epps's Scrapbook, 40, newspaper clipping dated 1 June 1925, "Big Crowd Sees 'Midget' Plane in Trial Flight."

[4] Ibid.

[5] Ibid.

[6] Ibid.

[7] Ibid, 51, "For Sale Ad" clipped from newspaper with handwritten date of 11 January 1926. The plane was listed for $1,000.00. See also Galt, "Epps," *Georgia Biography*, 294; Lola Trammell, ""Man Who Put Georgia in the Air,"Georgia in the Air," *Atlanta Journal Magazine*, 27 March 1949, 9; "Ben Epps: Athenian Was Pioneer Georgia Aviator," *Athens* (GA) *Banner Herald & Daily News*, 29 February 1976, 12G.

[8] Weider History Group, "Bill Piper and the Piper Cubs," accessed 5 August 2015, http://www.historynet.com/bill-piper-and-the-piper-cubs.htm. The earliest version of the Piper Cub, the E-2, sold for years for the price of $1,325. See also National Aviation Hall of Fame, "William Piper, Sr.," http:///www.nationalaviation.org/piper-sr-william/

[9] Ibid.

[10] Ibid.

[11] "One Killed and Another Injured as Epps Plane Plunges to Ground Here," *Athens* (GA) *Banner-Herald*, 5 June 1925, 1. See also "1 Killed, 1 Injured in Airplane Crash," *Atlanta Constitution*, 5 June 1925, 1.

[12] Ibid.

[13] Ibid.

[14] "Tragic Death of Young Otis Camp in Airplane Wreck in Athens Thurs. Funeral Attended by Big Crowd," *Winder* (GA) *News*, 11 June 1925, 1.

[15] "1 Killed, 1 Injured in Airplane Crash," *Atlanta Constitution*, 5 June 1925, 1.

[16] "Epps Plane Plunges to Ground," 1. The article reported that this crash was the second serious crash Ben had been involved in. The first had occurred several years earlier in Macon, Georgia, but no one died in that accident. According to Omie, Ben's crash in Macon occurred when he was on his way to an airshow in Florida. Ben stopped for gas in Macon and crashed just after he was out of sight of the town. Ben told Omie he thought the fueling station in Macon had put cheap gas in his plane, which caused the crash. Sadie B. Hornsby, "An Air-Minded Family," *Athens Memories, The WPA Federal Writers' Project Interviews*, ed. Al Hester (Athens, GA: The Green Berry Press, 2001) 26.

[17] "Tragic Death of Young Otis Camp in Airplane Wreck in Athens Thurs. Funeral Attended by Big Crowd," *Winder* (GA) *News*, 11 June 1925, 1.

[18] "Ben Epps Shows Steady Gain in Fight for Life," *Athens* (GA) *Banner-Herald*, 8 June 1925, 1.

[19] Epps Family Cousins Club, accessed 5 August 2015, http://reocities.com/Heartland/oaks/4050/epps.htm.

[20] Hornsby, "Air-Minded Family," *Athens Memories*, 20; Hargrett, Epps Papers, Box 5:3—Ben Epps Project 2001: interview of Virginia "Jenny" Epps Whitaker, Ben's daughter; "Mrs. Ben Epps Dies, Rites to Be Wednesday," *Athens* (GA) *Banner-Herald*, 20 June 1965, 1.

[21] Hornsby, "Air-Minded Family," *Athens Memories*, 20.

[22] Ibid.

[23] Warranty Deed from George M. Abney to Ben T. Epps, dated 21 January 1929, for Lot 11, Block 1, Lynwood Park, Clarke County, Clerk of Superior Court's Office, Athens, Georgia, Deed Book 51, page 570. According to this deed Ben gave $700 consideration for the lot.

[24] *Athens* (GA) *City Directory*, 1931.

[25] Epps Papers, Hargrett Library, Box 5, Folder 5:3, Ben Epps Project 2001: interview of Virginia "Jenny" Epps Whitaker.

[26] Hornsby, "Air-Minded Family," *Athens Memories*, 13.

[27] "The Birth of Aviation in Athens...Twenty Years Ago," *Athens* (GA) *Banner-Herald*, 4 August 1929, 1.

Chapter 12
[1] Epps Papers, Hargrett Library, Epps's Scrapbook, 64. Newspaper clipping, Bill Tyus, "13-Year-Old Boy *Flies* Plane," 8 December 1929.

[2] "Ben Epps Back from Air Race," *Athens* (GA) *Banner-Herald*, 7 September 1926, 8. Doug finished the race in fourth place.

[3] "When Chilled Steel Nerve, Strong Arm and Sure Eye Are Necessary," *Athens* (GA) *Banner-Herald*, 30 December 1926, 1; "Condition of the Weather Halted Arrival of Flyers," *Athens* (GA) *Banner-Herald*, 2 January 1927, 1.

[4] Epps Papers, Hargrett Library, Box 5, Folder 5:3, Ben Epps Project 2001: interview of Ben, Jr.

[5] Ibid., interview of Virginia "Jenny" Epps Whitaker. See also History of Air Racing and Record Breaking Pilots, "Doug Davis," accessed 5 August 2015, http://www.air-racing-history.com/PILOTS/Doug%20Davis.htm. In 1921, the Curtiss Candy Company of Chicago reconfigured its Kandy Kake into the Baby Ruth.

[6] Epps Papers, Hargrett Library, Epps's Scrapbook, 64. Newspaper clipping, Bill Tyus, "13-Year-Old Boy *Flies* Plane," 8 December 1929.

[7] Epps Papers, Hargrett Library, Box 1, Folder 1:12 Writings—Reminiscences of Ben Epps, Jr., #6.

[8] Ibid.

[9] "Boy, 13, Makes Solo Flight," *Atlanta Georgian & News*, 12 November 1929, 3.

[10] "Youngest Aviator to Fly at Air Races Here," *Atlanta Constitution*, 3 November 1929, 16A.

[11] "Boy, 13, Makes Solo Flight," 3.

[12] Sadie B. Hornsby, "An Air-Minded Family," *Athens Memories, The WPA Federal Writers' Project Interviews*, ed. Al Hester (Athens, GA: The Green Berry Press, 2001) 21.

[13] *Atlanta Journal*, 19 October 1930, Photogravure Section.

[14] Valco Lyle, "Georgia's Aviation Family," *Atlanta Constitution*, 6 July 1930, 7; Valco Lyle, "Georgia's Aviation Family," *Athens* (GA) *Banner-Herald*, 22 September 1930, 1. The article is accompanied by a photograph of a proud father, Evelyn, and Ben, Jr., standing in front of Ben's Waco 9.

[15] Ibid.

[16] Epps Papers, Hargrett Library, Epps's Scrapbook, 76. Newspaper clipping, "Floyd Gibbons of Radio Fame Tells World of Flying Epps Family Here." Gibbons was posthumously awarded a gold medal by the Marine Corps League, making him an honorary member of the Marine Corps. This was the first time a civilian ever received such an honor in the history of the Marine Corps League. Gibbons also received a star on the Hollywood Walk of Fame. See Radio Days website, accessed 7 August 2015, www.otr.com/gibbons.shtml; www.worldwar1.com/sffgbw.htm; Edward Gibbons, *Floyd Gibbons—Your Headline Hunter* (New York: Exposition Press 1953).

[17] Gibbons's letter in response to Ben's 26 September 1930 letter is at Epps Papers, Hargrett Library, Epps's Scrapbook, 76, letter dated 25 October 1930.

[18] Epps Papers, Hargrett Library, Epps's Scrapbook, 76. Newspaper clipping, "Floyd Gibbons of Radio Fame Tells World of Flying Epps Family Here."

[19] Edith Stearns Gray, *UP, A True Story of Aviation* (Strasburg, VA: Shenandoah Publishing House, 1931). The book also includes a photograph of Ben, Sr., and Ben, Jr., in front of the Waco. See also Epps Papers, Hargrett Library, Epps's Scrapbook, 63. Newspaper clipping, M. L. St. John, "Athens Boy Makes History as 'Up,' Story of Aviation, Comes Off Press."

[20] Epps Papers, Hargrett Library, Epps's Scrapbook, 84. Undated letter, signed "Junior."

[21] "Youngest Flyer Meets Hoover," *Dublin* (GA) *Courier-Herald*, 24 June 1931, 2.

[22] Epps Papers, Hargrett Library, Epps's Scrapbook, 85, letter dated 12 June 1931.

[23] Epps Papers, Hargrett Library, Epps's Scrapbook, 86, letter dated 11 June 1931.

[24] *Ben Epps, The Legacy of Georgia's First Aviator*, DVD, written and produced by William J. Evelyn (Athens: University of Georgia, 2001).

[25] "Obituary Notices," *Athens* (GA) *Banner-Herald*, 26 September 2001, A-11. See also Kevin Conner, "Son of flying pioneer, Ben T. Epps, Jr., dies," ibid, A-7. Ben Epps, Jr., died on 24 September 2001 in Atlanta. He had been enshrined in the Georgia Aviation Hall of Fame 7 May 1994. Ibid.

[26] Epps Papers, Hargrett Library, Box 5, Folder 5:3, Ben Epps Project 2001: interview of Virginia "Jenny" Epps Whitaker. The Naval Air Station in Atlanta became DeKalb-Peachtree Airport.

[27] Epps Papers, Hargrett Library, Box 5, Folder 5:3, Ben Epps Project 2001: interview of Loyd Florence. Florence lived in Athens and was executive vice-president of Fowler Products, which manufactured and rebuilt soft-drink equipment.

[28] "About Us," Epps Aviation, accessed 6 August 2015, http://www.eppsaviation.com/about/pat-epps-bio/.

Chapter 13

[1] "Alexander Eaglerock," The Museum of Flight, accessed 5 August 2015: http://www.museumofflight.org; Donald M. Pattillo, *A History in the Making, 80 Turbulent Years in the American General Aviation Industry* (New York: McGraw-Hill Co., 1998).

[2] There is no documentation about where Ben obtained the Ford Model "A" airplane engine. Ford did not sell airplane engines. An article that appeared in *Popular Aviation*, however, may provide a clue: The August 1930 edition of this magazine contained an article about two mechanical engineers from Dayton, Ohio, who designed an aviation motor using a Ford Model "A" motor and were offering the new design for sale. The engine was described as "light, well-designed, and sturdy." "Converted Ford Motor on Market," *Popular Science*, 7/1 (30 August 1930): 46.

[3] "Alexander Eaglerock," The Museum of Flight, accessed 5 August 2015, http://www.museumofflight.org/aircraft/alexander-eaglerock.

[4] Epps Papers, Hargrett Library, Epps's Scrapbook, 65. Blue pen notes at top of photograph of 1930 Epps XII Light Biplane read, "Epps Light BiPlane Tested Friday June 13, 1930, Model A Ford Motor" (Image Number 37).

[5] "Altitude Record Is Set by Epps Here Yesterday," *Athens* (GA) *Banner-Herald*, 20 March 1931, 8.

[6] Ibid.

[7] "Roy B. Epps Dies at Hospital Here; Funeral Tomorrow," *Athens* (GA) *Banner-Herald*, 15 March 1931, 1. At his death, Roy Epps was the proprietor of Athens Battery Co. and Mutual Service Station.

[8] Epps Papers, Hargrett Library, Epps's Scrapbook, 69. Newspaper clipping, "Ben Epps, Local Aviator, Gets Writeup in National Aeronautical Publication," citing the article by Manly Mills in *Popular Aviation*.

[9] Ibid.

[10] Advertisement, *Athens* (GA) *Banner-Herald*, 5 September 1928, 7; Advertisement, *Athens* (GA) *Banner-Herald*, 9 September 1928, 5.

[11] M. L. St. John, "Athens Takes to Aviation as Classes at Airport Here Grow," *Athens Banner-Herald*, 3 May 1931, 1.

[12] Epps Papers, Hargrett Library, Epps's Scrapbook, 109. Two newspaper clippings: "Georgia Coed Is First Woman to Solo in Athens" and "University of Georgia Ladybird."

[13] Ibid.

[14] "Plane Has Ground Wreck, Damaged; Also Automobiles," *Athens* (GA) *Banner-Herald*, 11 September 1928, 3.

[15] "Military Rites to Be Held for Army Air Hero," *Red and Black*, 24 March 1933, 1.

[16] "Hamilton Is Candidate for Airplane License," *Red and Black*, 10 April 1931, 5.

[17] Epps Papers, Hargrett Library, Epps's Scrapbook, 94. Newspaper clipping, "Athens Army Aviator Killed in Canal Zone," 15 March 1933.

[18] Epps Papers, Hargrett Library, Epps's Scrapbook, 79.

[19] "Military Rites to Be Held for Army Air Hero," *Red and Black*, 24 March 1933, 1.

[20] Epps Papers, Hargrett Library, Epps's Scrapbook, 95.

[21] "Son of Mr. and Mrs. B. T. Epps Dies; Accidentally Hurt," *Athens* (GA) *Banner-Herald*, 1 June 1932, 1. The accident occurred when Ben, Jr., backed the automobile out of the driveway and did not know his brother was behind it.

[22] Epps Papers, Hargrett Library, Epps's Scrapbook, 94. Newspaper clipping, "Athens Army Aviator Killed in Canal Zone," 15 March 1933.

[23] "Military Rites to Be Held for Army Air Hero," *Red and Black*, 24 March 1933, 1.

[24] Epps Papers, Hargrett Library, Epps's Scrapbook, 93, 94.

[25] "Davis, Douglas H.," Georgia Aviation Hall of Fame, plaque; Epps Papers, Hargrett Library, Epps's Scrapbook, 98, newspaper clipping, "Death Catches Douglas Davis in Speed Crash."

[26] Epps Papers, Hargrett Library, Epps's Scrapbook, 42 (Image Number 39).

[27] "Davis, Douglas H.," Georgia Aviation Hall of Fame, plaque.

[28] Epps Papers, Hargrett Library, Epps's Scrapbook, 108. Newspaper article clipped out of an unidentified newspaper titled, "Doings at the Y," by Dick Wade. The year "1934" is written in ink on the clipping.

[29] Sadie B. Hornsby, "An Air-Minded Family," *Athens Memories, The WPA Federal Writers' Project Interviews*, ed. Al Hester (Athens, GA: The Green Berry Press, 2001) 25.

[30] "Savannah Girl Killed Sunday in Plane Crash, Two Injured," *Red and Black*, 8 March 1935, 1.

[31] "Girl Dies in Plane Crash Here," *Athens* (GA) *Banner-Herald*, 4 March 1935, 1. The statement was attributed to K. O. Franks, "former boxing promoter and U.S. Army man." Ibid.

[32] Ibid. John Gordon, "a university student" and E. R. Durham, "who live[d] near the scene of the accident."

[33] The plane landed in the backyard of Burke Betts. The *Athens* (GA) *City Directory*, 1937, lists Betts's residence as 360 S. Lumpkin Street. See also "Airplane Crash Here Proves Fatal to Savannah Girl," *Athens* (GA) *Banner-Herald*, 5 March 1935, 1, which has a photograph of the crashed plane; "Airplane Crash, Near Campus, in Which University Visitor Met Death," *Red and Black*, 8 March 1935, 1. Other photographs of the crashed plane can be viewed at Epps Papers, Hargrett, Folder 1:8A, Photographs, Epps (Ben) plane crash 1937 [*sic*], photographs taken by R. P. Saye of 1935 crash near Lumpkin Street (Image Number 40).

[34] Ibid. According to Dr. Weyman Davis, Miss Raskin was dead when she arrived at the hospital, having "suffered a frontal skull fracture, itself sufficient to cause death; broken or dislocated right ankle and a compound fracture of the left leg." Ibid.

[35] "Plane Crash Kills Girl," *New York Times*, 4 March 1935.

[36] "Girl Dies in Plane Crash Here," *Athens* (GA) *Banner-Herald*, 4 March 1935, 1.

[37] *Athens* (GA) *Banner-Herald*, 6 March 1935, 2.

[38] *Athens* (GA) *Banner-Herald*, 8 March 1935, 6.

[39] Evelyn Epps Galt, "Epps, Benjamin Thomas," in *Dictionary of Georgia Biography*, vol. 1, eds. Kenneth Coleman and Charles Stephen Gurr (Athens: University of Georgia Press, 1983) 294.

[40] Ibid.

[41] Epps Papers, Hargrett Library, Box 5, Folder 5:3, Ben Epps Project 2001: interview of Ben Epps, Jr.

[42] Epps Papers, Hargrett Library, Box 5, Folder 5:3, Ben Epps Project 2001: interview of Ben Epps, Jr.

[43] *Athens* (GA) *City Directory*, 1937. The Federal Building Warehouse was located at 160-170 W. Broad Street.

[44] Hornsby, "Air-Minded Family," *Athens Memories*, 27.

[45] Epps Papers, Hargrett Library, Epps's Scrapbook, 105. Letter dated 6 July 1937 from Montgomery School of Aeronautics to Ben Epps confirming the sale of its Waco 10 to Ben for cash and Ben's OX5 Travelair.

[46] Galt, "Epps," *Georgia Biography*, 294.

[47] Epps Papers, Hargrett Library, Box 5, Folder 5:3, Ben Epps Project 2001: interview of Loyd Florence.

[48] "Ben Epps Dies Last Night of Plane Crash Injuries Sustained Here Saturday," *Athens* (GA) *Banner-Herald*, 17 October 1937, 1. There is a photograph of Ben's crashed Gipsy de Havilland biplane taken by Kenneth Kay in the *Atlanta Georgian & News*, 18 October 1937, 2. Kay's photograph also appears, courtesy of the *Atlanta Georgian & News*, in the *Athens* (GA) *Banner-Herald*, 19 October 1937, 2.

[49] Ibid.

[50] Ibid.

[51] *Ben Epps, The Legacy of Georgia's First Aviator*, DVD, written and produced by William J. Evelyn (Athens, GA: University of Georgia, 2001).; Epps Papers, Hargrett Library, Box 5, Folder 5:3, Ben Epps Project 2001.

[52] Hornsby, "Air-Minded Family," *Athens Memories*, 27–28.

[53] Ibid., 14, 17, 29.

[54] Ibid., 23–24.

[55] Epps Papers, Hargrett Library, Box 5, Folder 5:3, Ben Epps Project 2001: interview of Loyd Florence and interview of Virginia "Jenny" Epps Whitaker.

[56] Hornsby, "Air-Minded Family," *Athens Memories*, 17

[57] Ibid., 25.

[58] "Diligent Search for Assailants of W. C. Wright," *Atlanta Constitution*, 5 March 1925, 1; "Wright's Car Found in Athens; 2 Suspects

Sought," *Atlanta Journal*, 5 March 1925, 1; "Three Youthful Suspects in Attack on W. C. Wright Rushed Here for Safety," *Atlanta Journal*, 6 March 1925, 1; "Signed Confession Made by One of Youths Who Slugged and Robbed Professor Wright," *Atlanta Constitution*, 8 March 1925, 1; "Funeral Sunday in Eatonton," *Atlanta Constitution*, 8 March 1925, 10. The three men, ages 20, 20, and 19 were hitchhiking from Tampa, Florida, to Ohio to find work. Wright stopped to pick up two of them, who had Wright drive to where the third was hiding. Wright was struck in the head eleven times with a tire spring and left to die. Ironically, the three drove Wright's car into Clarke County and abandoned it behind a church on Epps Mill Road. The three were arrested on 5 March outside of Danielsville, Georgia. One of the attackers signed a confession. The other two were tried, convicted of murder by a jury, and sentenced to die in the electric chair. The conviction was appealed and subsequently upheld by the Georgia Supreme Court. Their execution date was reset and they were put to death in the electric chair in March 1926. From the date they were arrested, it was only twelve months before their execution was carried out, which included a two-month stay of the execution. "Coggeshall and McClelland Electrocuted Tuesday, Mar. 23 at State Prison for Foul Murder of Prof. W. C. Wright," *Eatonton* (GA) *Messenger*, 26 March 1926, 1.

[59] M. L. St. John, "Athens Takes to Aviation as Classes at Airport Here Grow," *Athens* (GA) *Banner-Herald*, 3 May 1931, 1.

[60] Epps Papers, Hargrett Library, Epps's Scrap Book, 96. Letter dated 17 November 1937 from Bernard F. Freeman addressed to "Mrs. Epps and Family."

[61] Ibid.

[62] Hornsby, "Air-Minded Family," 28.

[63] Ibid., 17.

[64] Epps Papers, Hargrett Library, Box 5, Folder 5:3, Ben Epps Project 2001: interview of Loyd Florence.

[65] "Mrs. Ben Epps Dies; Rites to Be Wednesday," *Athens* (GA) *Banner-Herald*, 20 June 1965, 1.

Epilogue
[1] George Bernard Shaw, *Back to Methuselah (A Metabiological Pentateuch)* (New York: Brentano's, 1921). Found in, "In the Beginning: B.C. 4004 in the Garden of Eden."

---

[2] "Hartsfield-Jackson Atlanta International Airport," accessed 1 August 2015, http://www.atlanta-airport.com/Airport/ATL/ATL_FactSheet.aspx; see also, "World Airport Codes," accessed 1 August 2015, http://www.world-airport-codes.com/world-top-30-airports.html.

[3] Epps Papers, Hargrett Library, Box 5, Folder 5:3, Ben Epps Project 2001: interview of Ben, Jr., shortly before his death in September 2001. When asked what his father would have considered his greatest achievement, Ben, Jr., answered, "His family."

Index

INDEX

INDEX